CASSEROLES STEWS & HOTPOTS

Bay Books Sydney and London

CONTENTS

Publisher: George Barber

Published in 1984 by Bay Books Pty Ltd
61–69 Anzac Parade, Kensington,
NSW 2033 Australia

National Library of Australia
Card Number and ISBN 0 85835 554 X

INTRODUCTION

A rich beef stew can be made from these flavorsome ingredients

Casseroles, stews and hotpots — easy to make and delicious to eat — provide the perfect answer for many occasions, from family meals to special dinner parties. Meat, poultry, fish or vegetables can be used as the basis for these three slightly different types of cooking. Perhaps the greatest advantage of these versatile dishes is that they can be cooked well in advance and need little or no last-minute attention other than reheating.

Casseroles differ from stews in that they are cooked in the oven rather than on top of the stove and need much less liquid than either stews or hotpots. They are usually made with the better cuts of meat, such as round steak or chops — and so need less cooking time than stews. Traditionally, a casserole is served in the dish in which it is cooked. The most convenient type of casserole dish is one that is flameproof as well as ovenproof. This feature enables you to brown the meat or poultry on top of the stove before placing the dish in the oven. It also means the casserole can be reheated on the stove, making it easier to adjust the thickening if necessary.

Stews generally use the least expensive cuts of meat such as chuck steak, oxtail, lamb neck chops or veal knuckles. These require a long, slow cooking process. The gentle simmering not only tenderises the meat, but brings out its rich flavours and aromas. Ideally, stews are cooked in plenty of liquid in a heavy cast-iron pot. Like many casseroles, their flavour improves if cooked a day or two ahead allowing the sauce to continue its work of tenderising as it cools.

There are several different types of stew. A white stew is called a fricassee. Unlike the better-known brown stew — where the meat is well seared before adding the stock and other ingredients — the meat of a white stew is first blanched in boiling water and then placed directly into the cooking pot.

An everyday stew can be turned simply into a special party dish by adding cream or wine. It can easily take on a gala appearance when garnished with parsley or sprigs of fresh herbs, surrounded with creamed potatoes, fluffy white rice or noodles, and served on a large, warmed dish.

A hotpot, unlike a casserole or a stew, is cooked in a clear stock and has no thickening agent other than the starch in potatoes, beans or lentils if they are used. Many hotpots, especially those originating from Middle Eastern or

African countries, are served by spoon so that full advantage can be taken of the deliciously rich gravy.

The liquid used in most casseroles, stews and hotpots is based on beef or chicken stock, which can easily be made from bouillon cubes. This ready-made stock is a boon for today's busy cooks. Remember when using the cubes, however, that they are already well seasoned, so never add salt to your dish until you have first checked the seasoning. For special occasions it is well worthwhile to make your own stock. Beef bones, a stalk or two of celery, a small carrot and onion, a bouquet garni and half a dozen peppercorns, gently simmered in water for a few hours will give a rich flavourful broth. For chicken stock, substitute a chicken carcass for the beef bones.

Many of the recipes in this book include a bouquet garni. If you can obtain fresh herbs make up a small bunch of parsley, thyme, basil and marjoram (or whatever is at hand), and tie together with string. If these are unavailable, use dried bouquet garni mixtures now available commercially in small muslin bags.

NOTE When using liquids and needing to convert cup and spoon quantities to metric equivalents, use the following measures:

1 cup = 250 mL
1 tablespoon = 20 mL
1 teaspoon = 5 mL

Beef Niçoise (See page 10)

BEEF

Beef is the basic ingredient of some of the most famous of all casserole dishes — the *daubes* of France. Braised in red wine stock and well seasoned with herbs, dishes such as Boeuf en Daube and Pot au Feu are delicious and wonderfully aromatic.

In all the recipes — from traditional English stews to exotic Mediterranean dishes — the emphasis is on flavour. The long, slow cooking process, the natural high flavour of stewing cuts of beef and the imaginative use of herbs, spices and stock ensures a feast for the taste buds.

Pot au Feu (*See page* 18)

Beef and Eggplant Casserole

Serves 6

1 kg stewing beef, such as chuck steak
1 teaspoon paprika
¼ cup oil
1 cup chick peas, canned *or* ½ cup dried chick peas
3 cloves garlic
2 large onions
2 tablespoons tomato paste
4 cups water
4 medium eggplants
salt, pepper
oil for deep frying

Note If using dried chick peas, soak them overnight in water

Trim any excess fat from the meat and cut into large cubes. Heat oil in a large flameproof dish and fry meat quickly until well browned on all sides. Sprinkle the paprika over the meat and stir. When the meat pieces are brown spoon out any excess oil and add drained chick peas, crushed garlic, peeled and chopped onions, tomato paste and water. Bring to the boil, cover and simmer gently for 2–2½ hours or until meat is tender.

Meanwhile slice the eggplants, place on a dish or wooden board and sprinkle liberally with salt. Leave for 30 minutes, then rinse and dry the slices. Heat oil in a deep pan and deep fry the eggplant slices until golden. Drain on absorbent paper.

Add the cooked eggplant slices to the beef casserole and season to taste with salt and pepper. Simmer for another 30 minutes. Serve direct from the casserole or in a heated serving dish. The casserole should contain plenty of richly flavoured liquid which may be eaten with a spoon, like a soup.

Beef and Cider Hotpot

Serves 4

750g topside steak
3 tablespoons butter or margarine
1 large onion
2 large carrots
2 turnips
4 tablespoons flour
2 full cups apple cider
salt and pepper
1 beef stock cube
500g potatoes
¾ cup grated cheese

Trim and cut steak into thin slices. Peel and slice onion and carrots; peel and chop turnips. Heat butter in a heavy pan and brown the beef slices. Remove. Add onion, carrots and turnips to pan and fry gently for 10 minutes. Stir in flour. Remove pan from heat and gradually pour in the cider, combining thoroughly. Return pan to heat and continue stirring until mixture boils and thickens. Then add crumbled stock cube and seasoning to taste. Simmer for 5 minutes.

Transfer beef and the vegetable mixture to an ovenproof dish. Peel and slice potatoes and arrange on top. Cover and cook in a moderate oven for 1½–2 hours. Sprinkle grated cheese on top, raise oven temperature to moderately hot and cook uncovered for about 15 minutes or until the cheese is golden brown.

Beef Goulash

Serves 4

750g chuck or blade steak
2 tablespoons oil
3 medium-sized onions
1 tablespoon paprika
good pinch cumin
2 cloves garlic, crushed
salt and pepper
pinch marjoram
3 tomatoes
1 green pepper
2½ cups water
½ cup dry red wine
2 beef stock cubes
3 tablespoons cornflour
4 tablespoons water, extra
4 tablespoons sour cream

Trim steak and cut into 2.5cm pieces. Thinly slice onions, seed and chop pepper, skin and chop tomatoes.

Heat oil in heavy pan and fry onions until golden brown, about 4 minutes. Add meat and cook gently for 8 minutes, stirring from time to time. Add paprika, cumin, garlic, seasoning and marjoram and cook for 1 minute more. Add tomatoes and green pepper and simmer for another 10 minutes. Stir in the wine and water and crumble in stock cubes. Cover and cook gently for 1½ hours or until meat is tender. When

Beef and Cider Hotpot

ready to serve dissolve cornflour in water, stir into meat and cook for 2–3 minutes, stirring until thickened.

Place a dollop of sour cream on top of each serving of goulash. Boiled new potatoes is a traditional accompaniment but noodles or fluffy rice, flecked with chopped parsley, can be served in place of the potatoes, if preferred.

Beef Nicoise

Serves 6

1 kg chuck steak
100 g lean bacon
2 tablespoons oil
4 onions
2 cloves garlic
1 bouquet garni
4 tablespoons flour
1 ¼ cups dry red wine
1 ¼ cups water
1 beef stock cube
1 ½ tablespoons tomato paste
6 tomatoes
salt and pepper
1 tablespoon chopped parsley
6 black olives

Cut the meat into 2.5 cm cubes and chop bacon into large pieces. Heat oil in heavy pan and brown beef and bacon for 8 minutes, covered with a lid. Stir often. Add peeled and sliced onion, crushed garlic and bouquet garni and cook for 4 minutes. Sprinkle on the flour, combine and cook for 1 minute.

Turn off heat and gradually stir in the wine, water, crumbled stock cubes and skinned and chopped tomatoes. Return pan to heat and continue stirring until mixture boils. Add seasoning, cover and simmer for 1½–2 hours or until meat is tender. Mixture can be transferred to an ovenproof dish and cooked in a moderate oven with a lid on for the same time. Just before serving add chopped parsley and olives.

Beef Cobbler

Serves 4

750 g chuck or round steak
2 tablespoons oil
1 onion
1 carrot
½ cup flour
2 tablespoons tomato paste or purée
1 ¼ cups water
1 ¼ cups beer
1 beef stock cube
1 clove garlic
pinch rosemary
salt and pepper
1 tablespoon milk
1 tablespoon chopped parsley

Cobbler topping:

1 ½ cups self-raising flour
pinch salt
2 stalks celery, chopped
2 tablespoons chopped parsley
3 tablespoons butter or margarine
½ cup milk

Cut steak into 2.5 cm cubes. Heat the oil in a pan and brown the meat pieces. Add the peeled and chopped onion and carrot and cook for 2 or 3 minutes. Stir in the flour and cook for a further minute. Add the tomato paste or purée, water and beer and crumble in the stock cube. Add crushed garlic and rosemary and keep stirring until the mixture boils. Simmer for another three minutes. Transfer to a casserole dish, cover and cook in a moderate oven for 1 ½ hours, or until meat is tender.

Meanwhile make the cobbler topping. Mix together the flour, salt, celery and parsley in a bowl. Rub in the butter until the mixture resembles fine breadcrumbs. Add the milk, a little at a time, and mix well to make a soft dough. Knead the dough lightly on a floured board and roll out 2 cm thick. Using a 7 cm cutter, cut out as many circles as you can. Then, using a 1 cm cutter, cut a hole in the centre of each dough circle.

Remove the casserole from the oven and season to taste. Increase oven temperature to moderately hot. Arrange the scone rings, overlapping in a circle, around the top of the casserole and brush with milk. When oven is at required temperature return the casserole and bake a further 20 minutes until the topping is golden brown. Before serving garnish with chopped parsley.

Beef Cobbler, Quick Beef and Chicken Casserole (See page 18) and Mexican Hotpot (See page 12

French Beef and Bean Hotpot

Serves 6

750g stewing beef
2 tablespoons oil
2 large onions
1 clove garlic
2 tablespoons flour
1 tablespoon tomato paste
1¼ cups water
½ cup white wine
1 bouquet garni
sprig rosemary
salt, pepper
250g butter beans or lima beans
2 zucchini, sliced
4 tomatoes

Note If using dried beans, soak them overnight in water, then bring to boil and simmer for 1 hour or until tender. Rinse and drain.

Trim fat from meat and cut into 2.5cm cubes. Heat oil in pan and brown meat pieces. Add the peeled and chopped onion and crushed garlic and cook for 2 minutes. Sprinkle in the flour and cook for 2 minutes to brown it. Stir in the tomato paste, then gradually pour in the water and wine, stirring constantly until mixture boils. Season with bouquet garni, rosemary, salt and pepper and simmer for 10 minutes.

Transfer the mixture to an ovenproof dish. Add the beans, cover, and bake in a moderate oven for 1½–2 hours.

Remove the hotpot from the oven, add sliced zucchini and quartered tomatoes, and return to oven for 15 minutes. Check seasoning and serve hot.

Mexican Hotpot

Serves 4

500g minced steak
2 tablespoons oil
1 large onion
1 green pepper
1 red pepper
pinch paprika
pinch chilli powder
4 tablespoons flour
2 tablespoons tomato paste
1¾ cups water
1 beef stock cube
1 bouquet garni
salt and pepper
1 cup canned or cooked dried kidney beans

Heat the oil in a saucepan and fry chopped onion until soft. Add the seeded and chopped peppers and cook for 1 minute. Add minced steak and cook for about 5 minutes or until meat browns, stirring occasionally.

Stir in the paprika, chilli powder and flour. Combine well and cook for 2 minutes. Turn off heat and stir in the tomato paste; crumble in the stock cube and gradually add the water. Return pan to heat and continue stirring until the mixture boils. Add the bouquet garni, lower heat and cook gently on top of stove for 30 minutes. Season with salt and pepper to taste and add the drained kidney beans. Continue cooking for another 5 minutes until the beans are heated through. Serve with boiled rice.

For a more authentic South American flavour increase the amount of chilli powder and add a cup of canned corn kernels.

Boeuf à la mode

Serves 8

1.5kg round steak, in one piece
8 carrots, sliced thinly
1 onion, chopped finely
1 bay leaf
½ teaspoon dried thyme
3 sprigs parsley
¼ teaspoon salt
freshly ground black pepper
1½ cups red wine
2 tablespoons olive oil or vegetable oil
3 onions, finely chopped
4 cloves garlic
12 large mushrooms, chopped
1 teaspoon lemon juice
250g bacon
½ cup beef stock
3 tablespoons flour

Place carrots, onion, bay leaf, thyme and parsley, salt and pepper in a bowl. Add the beef and wine. Cover and marinate the beef in the refrigerator for 24 hours, turning every 8 hours. Remove the meat. Dry on paper towels. Strain and reserve the marinade.

Heat the oil in a heavy casserole and brown the meat on all sides over high heat. Lower the heat and fry onions and garlic in the same oil for 3 minutes. Add mushrooms and lemon juice and continue cooking for

Beef Goulash (*See page* 8)

5 minutes. In the meantime, fry bacon until almost crisp. Drain and leave to one side. Heat reserved marinade with beef stock. Stir flour into onions and mushrooms. Add bacon. Replace beef in the casserole and stir in warm wine and stock. Cover and cook 2½ hours in a moderate oven.

Beef and Olive Casserole

Serves 6

1 kg chuck or topside steak
30g butter or margarine
1 tablespoon oil
2 small to medium onions
4 carrots
2 stalks celery
1 clove garlic
4 tablespoons flour
1¼ cups water
½ cup sherry
400g can of tomatoes
1 beef stock cube
bay leaf
few sprigs of parsley
salt, pepper
6 stuffed green olives

Trim any surplus fat off meat and cut into 4 cm cubes. Heat butter and oil in a pan and sauté meat pieces until well browned. Drain and transfer to casserole dish.

Add peeled and sliced carrots, sliced celery, quartered onions and crushed garlic to the pan and fry over low heat for about 5 minutes. Stir in flour and cook gently for a few minutes. Gradually add the combined water, sherry, undrained tomatoes and crumbled stock cube stirring well until the mixture boils and thickens. Add bay leaf and parsley and season with salt and pepper. Pour the vegetables and the sauce over the meat in the casserole. Cover, and cook in a moderate oven for 2–2½ hours or until meat is tender. Remove bay leaf and parsley. Stir in the sliced olives and serve with French beans and boiled potatoes.

Beef and Olive Casserole

Russian Beef Casserole with Caraway Rice (See page 16)

wines are
cool controlled
Die Keldermeester van Die
bosch, berei wyne vir die
alleenlik van uitstaande
Suid-Afrika se
word hierdie wyne in Die
in koel en ideale

Hungarian Meatballs

Serves 4

500 g minced steak
½ cup fresh breadcrumbs
1 egg
salt and pepper
1 tablespoon chopped parsley
flour
2 tablespoons oil
3 large onions
1 tablespoon paprika
3 tablespoons tomato paste
2 tablespoons flour, extra
1 beef stock cube
1¼ cups water
¼ teaspoon caraway seeds (optional)
500 g potatoes

Mix the minced meat, breadcrumbs, lightly whisked egg, salt and pepper and parsley in a bowl. Shape about 12 meatballs and lightly dust with flour. Heat oil in a pan, brown the meatballs and transfer them to casserole.

Slice onions, add a little more oil to the pan if necessary, and fry onions until they are golden brown. Add the paprika and tomato paste and cook for 2 minutes. Sprinkle on the 2 tablespoons flour, stir in and cook for 1 minute. Turn off heat and add the water and stock cube which has been dissolved in a little boiling water. Return pan to heat and continue stirring until sauce boils and thickens. Season and add caraway seeds. Pour sauce over meatballs. Peel and thinly slice potatoes and arrange around the dish. Bake in moderate oven for 45 minutes.

Russian Beef Casserole with Caraway Rice

Serves 6

1 kg chuck or blade steak
2 tablespoons oil
3 stalks celery
1 large onion
150 mL water
1 beef stock cube
450 g can pineapple pieces
1 tablespoon chopped parsley
¼ teaspoon sugar
1 tablespoon tomatoe paste or purée
½ teaspoon Worcestershire sauce
salt and pepper

Trim fat from the steak and cut into 2.5 cm cubes. Heat oil in pan, add meat pieces and brown well on all sides. Transfer meat to a casserole dish. Slice celery, peel and chop onion and fry for 3 minutes. Drain and add to the casserole.

Pour the water into a clean pan, bring to the boil and crumble in the stock cube. Drain pineapple and add the juice to the stock with parsley, sugar, tomatoe paste, Worcestershire sauce and salt and pepper to taste. Pour sauce over meat and vegetables and cover casserole. Cook in a moderate oven for 1½ hours or until meat is tender, adding more stock if necessary. Fifteen minutes before the end of cooking, add pineapple pieces.

Caraway Rice: Cook 1½ cups long grain rice in a large saucepan of salted boiling water. Boil for 12 minutes or until rice is tender. Drain thoroughly. Gently stir in 2 tablespoons butter and 2 teaspoons caraway seeds. Serve with the casserole.

Boeuf en Daube

Serves 6

1 kg lean stewing steak
175 g bacon
350 mL red wine
75 g butter
250 g carrots, sliced
2 leeks, sliced
1 clove garlic, crushed
2 tomatoes, peeled and chopped
1 bouquet garni
450 g beef stock
150 g button onions, peeled
175 g button mushrooms
3 tablespoons oil
1 tablespoon chopped parsley

Remove excess fat from the steak and cut into cubes. Dice the bacon, place in a bowl with the steak and pour over the wine. Marinate for 3–4 hours.

Set the oven at 150°C (300°F). Remove the meat from the marinade. Melt half the butter and fry the meat until evenly browned. Remove from the pan. Melt the remaining butter and fry the carrots, leeks and garlic for 5 minutes. Stir in the tomatoes and season well. Place the meat and fried vegetables in an ovenproof casserole. Add the marinade and bouquet garni.

Pour the stock into the pan and bring to the boil, stirring well to loosen the sediment. Add to the casserole, cover and cook for 2¼ hours.

Fry the onions and mushrooms in the oil for 3 minutes. Add to the casserole, sprinkle with the parsley and cook for a further 45 minutes. Remove the bouquet garni and serve hot with creamed potatoes.

3eef in Red Wine

Serves 6

.5 kg topside or round steak
tablespoons oil
0 g butter
00 g rindless lean bacon
50 g mushrooms, thickly sliced
0 g butter, extra
clove garlic, crushed
½ tablespoons flour
½ cups burgundy or other dry red wine
½ cups water
beef stock cubes
bouquet garni
alt and pepper
2 tiny onions
scant tablespoon sugar
0 g butter, extra

Remove any fat from the steak and cut into 2.5 cm cubes. Heat butter and oil in a heavy pan, add meat pieces and brown over a high heat, stirring the pieces regularly. Remove meat, drain on absorbent paper and transfer to a casserole. Lightly fry the bacon, cut into strips; remove, drain and place in casserole with the meat. Fry the sliced mushrooms, stirring for 1 minute. Remove from pan and put aside.

Add the extra butter (60 g) to the pan and cook crushed garlic for 1 minute. Add the flour and lightly brown stirring constantly with a wooden spoon. Remove pan from heat. Gradually add the water and wine, stirring until smooth and well combined. Return pan to heat, add crumbled stock cubes and continue stirring until mixture boils and thickens. Add bouquet garni. Check seasoning (stock cubes are often salty) and add salt and pepper to taste. Pour the sauce over the meat. Cover casserole and cook in a moderate oven for 1 hour.

oeuf en Daube

Meanwhile place the small peeled onions in a saucepan with the sugar, butter (30g) and enough water to cover. Cook uncovered until water has evaporated and onions have softened. When a golden caramel mixture remains roll the onions in it and put to one side.

Remove the casserole from the oven at the end of 1 hour and stir in the onions and mushrooms. Cover the casserole and cook a further 30 minutes or until the meat is tender.

Quick Beef and Chicken Casserole

Serves 4

⅔ cup cooked beef, cut into strips
1¼ cups white sauce
¼ cup dry sherry
salt and pepper
1 gherkin
⅔ cup cooked chicken, diced
⅔ cup sliced mushrooms
⅔ cup ham, cut into strips
2 tablespoons flaked almonds

Heat the prepared white sauce and stir in sherry. Season with salt and pepper. Place the beef and sliced gherkin in the botton of an ovenproof dish. Pour in half the white sauce. Put a layer of chicken, mushrooms and half a cup of the ham on top. Pour over the remaining white sauce and sprinkle with the almonds and remaining ham strips.

Place in a moderate oven and warm through for 15 minutes. For extra body, mix in a small can of butter beans.

Oxtail Stew

Serves 6

1 kg oxtail, cut into pieces
½ cup flour
salt and pepper
3 tablespoons oil
1 large onion, sliced
2 large carrots, cut into pieces lengthways
2 turnips, cut into chunks
3 stalks of celery, thickly sliced
4 cups water
3 beef stock cubes
2 tablespoons tomato paste
1 bay leaf
1 bouquet garni
½ teaspoon oregano
salt and pepper to taste
1 tablespoon chopped parsley

Remove excess fat from the oxtail and toss in flour seasoned with salt and pepper. Heat oil in a large pan and brown the meat well. Remove from the pan, drain on absorbent paper and place in a large ovenproof casserole.

Lightly fry the sliced onions, carrot and turnip pieces and the sliced celery. Drain and transfer to the casserole.

In a separate saucepan combine the water, crumbled stock cubes, tomato paste, bay leaf, bouquet garni and oregano and bring to the boil. Check seasoning and add salt to taste and a good sprinkle of pepper. Pour this liquid over the meat and vegetables. Cover the casserole tightly and cook in a moderately slow oven for 3 hours. Allow to cool, then skim off the fat. If possible cool and chill overnight so that the fat sets firmly and is easy to remove.

Return the casserole to the oven for another hour before serving.

Pot au Feu

Serves 6

1.5kg round or chuck steak
2 marrow bones (optional)
1 teaspoon salt
10 peppercorns
½ teaspoon dried thyme
1 bay leaf
1 tablespoon chopped parsley
2 medium onions
4 cloves
2 stalks celery, sliced
250g carrots, sliced
250g turnips, cubed
2 leeks or ½ bunch shallots, sliced
250g potatoes, cubed
1 small cabbage, roughly cut
½ cup red wine
pickles
French mustard
coarse sea salt

Tie meat securely to maintain shape. Place the beef, marrow bones, salt, peppercorns, thyme, bay leaf and parsley in a heavy pan. Almost cover with water, bring to the boil and skim. Reduce the heat, partially cover and simmer for 2–2½ hours, skimming occasionally.

Spike one of the onions with the cloves and slice the other. Add these to the pot along with the celery, carrots, turnips, leeks and potatoes. Simmer, partially covered another hour. Add the cabbage and continue simmering for 30 minutes. Remove the meat and vegetables from the stock. Slice the meat and place on a platter with the vegetables.

If using marrow bones remove the marrow and spread on toasted French bread as an accompaniment; discard the bones.

Skim any fat from the stock, add the wine and transfer to a warm bowl. Serve the meat and vegetables from the platter and pass the stock, French bread, pickles, mustard and sea salt separately.

Beef Carbonade

Serves 4

[illegible]00g chuck steak
[illegible] tablespoons lard or dripping
[illegible] onions, sliced
[illegible] tablespoon flour
[illegible]00 mL beer
550 mL hot water
1 clove garlic, crushed
1 bouquet garni
pinch sugar
pinch nutmeg
1 teaspoon vinegar
6 × 5 mm thick slices French bread
2 tablespoons Dijon mustard

Set the oven at 170°C (325°F). Cut the meat into bite-sized pieces, discarding the excess fat. Heat the lard or dripping in a large pan, add the meat and fry quickly until browned. Stir in the onions and cook until golden.

Sprinkle the flour into the pan and add the beer, water, garlic, bouquet garni, sugar, nutmeg, vinegar and seasoning to taste. Bring to the boil, transfer to an ovenproof casserole and cover tightly with a lid.

Cook for 2 hours, then skim the surface and remove the bouquet garni. Spread the slices of bread with the mustard and arrange over the top of the casserole, pushing each slice below the surface so that it becomes soaked with gravy. Return the casserole to the oven and bake uncovered for a further 40 minutes, until the top is crusty and golden.

Serve piping hot, with vegetables or salad.

Oxtail Stew

LAMB

Traditionally, mutton or yearling rather than lamb has been used for casseroles and similar dishes. Unfortunately mutton is not generally available in butchers' shops these days, lamb having almost totally supplanted it in the market.

Lamb is more tender and delicately flavoured than mutton and it would be wise to bear this in mind when trying these recipes. The better cuts (such as leg and chump chops) in particular do not require the lengthy cooking time of some of the beef dishes.

Barley and Lamb Hotpot (*See page 22*

Barley and Lamb Hotpot

Serves 6

1 kg stewing lamb
1 parsnip
2 turnips
1 onion
2 carrots
2 stalks celery
6 cups water
1 bouquet garni
salt and pepper
90g barley
1 tablespoon chopped parsley

Soak barley overnight in cold water. Cut lamb into cubes and blanch in boiling water for 5 minutes. Rinse in cold water and drain.

Place the meat in a large saucepan, add diced parsnip, turnips, and carrots, chopped onion and celery, bouquet garni, salt and pepper. Pour in water and bring to the boil; simmer for 30 minutes.

Add the barley and simmer for 1 hour until meat and barley are tender, adding extra water if needed. Remove the bouquet garni and check the seasoning. Just before serving sprinkle with chopped parsley.

Carbonade of Lamb

Serves 4

4 slices lamb cut from top of leg across bone or 750g any lean lamb
2 tablespoons flour, seasoned with salt and pepper
2 tablespoons oil
2½ cups sliced onions
1 clove garlic
1 green pepper
500g tomatoes
2 carrots
salt and pepper
1 bouquet garni
1¼ cups dry white wine
1 teaspoon chopped parsley

Trim lamb, cut into large cubes or into 1.5cm slices. Toss in seasoned flour. Heat oil in pan, add meat, cover and fry gently for 4 minutes. Drain well and transfer to a casserole dish.

In the same pan gently fry the peeled and sliced onion until soft. Add crushed garlic, sliced and seeded green pepper and sliced carrots. Cover and cook on a low heat for 1 minute. Add salt and pepper, bouquet garni and gradually pour in the wine, stirring all the time. Boil for 5 minutes.

Pour the contents of the pan over the meat. Cover the casserole and bake in a moderately hot oven for 45–60 minutes. When meat is cooked there should be no more than 1 or 2 tablespoons liquid left in the casserole. Check the casserole while cooking to ensure that it does not dry out. Add extra wine if necessary.

Before serving, check the seasoning. Serve garnished with chopped parsley.

Lamb Curry

Serves 6

1 kg boned shoulder of lamb
2 tablespoons oil
2 large onions
2 tablespoons curry powder
1 tablespoon turmeric
1 teaspoon powdered ginger
150 mL beef stock
salt and pepper
1 tablespoon tomato paste
2 tablespoons mango chutney
2 tablespoons raisins
½ cup sour cream or yogurt
2 tablespoons slivered almonds
½ lemon

Cut the lamb into 2.5cm cubes. Heat the oil in a heavy pan, peel and slice the onions and fry until soft. Add lamb pieces and brown evenly. Stir in curry powder, turmeric and ginger and cook for 3 minutes. Stir in the stock and season with salt and pepper. Add tomato paste and bring to the boil, stirring all the time. Add mango chutney and raisins and simmer, covered, for 45 minutes or until the meat is tender. Then stir in the sour cream or yogurt and most of the almonds. Simmer gently for 10 more minutes.

Arrange the curry on a heated serving dish, surrounded by a ring of boiled rice. Sprinkle the remaining almonds on top of meat and decorate with lemon slices. Serve with sambals such as coconut, mango chutney, sliced tomatoes, bananas, chopped apple, cucumber and orange segments.

Lamb Curry

Dijon Hotpot

Serves 6

6 large lean lamb cutlets
2 tablespoons oil
2 stalks celery
4 carrots
1 swede
2 onions
1¼ cups water
½ cup dry white vermouth
pinch marjoram
pinch thyme
salt and pepper
pinch cumin
1 tablespoon honey
1 tablespoon vinegar
1 chicken stock cube
1 teaspoon Dijon mustard

Heat oil in a pan and fry the cutlets until browned. Drain and transfer to an ovenproof dish and cover with the sliced celery and carrots, chopped swede and onions. Pour in the water and vermouth. Sprinkle in herbs and season with salt and pepper. Stir in the cumin, honey and vinegar. Crumble in the stock cube. Cover with a lid and bake in moderate oven for 1½ hours until the meat is tender. Stir in the mustard and blend well with the hotpot liquid. Serve with boiled rice or potatoes.

Chump Chops Catalania

Serves

6 lamb chump chops
¼ cup seasoned flour
¼ cup oil
3 onions
4 tomatoes
1 clove garlic
150 mL white wine
150 mL water
1 chicken stock cube
salt and pepper
bouquet garni
4 zucchini
500g potatoes
150 mL white sauce
3 tablespoons Cheddar cheese

Dijon Hotpot

Chump Chops Catalania

Dredge chops in seasoned flour. Heat oil in a pan and fry the chops until well browned on both sides. Remove, drain, and arrange in the bottom of a shallow ovenproof dish. In the same oil, gently fry the sliced onions until they are transparent. Add skinned and chopped tomatoes and crushed garlic. Pour in the wine and water and crumble in the stock cube. Season with salt and pepper and add bouquet garni. Simmer for about 5 minutes.

Meanwhile blanch the sliced zucchini in boiling water for 2 or 3 minutes and arrange over the lamb chops in the dish. Pour the tomato and wine mixture over the top. Blanch the potatoes in boiling water for 4 minutes. Slice thinly and arrange them, overlapping, across the top of the dish.

Heat the white sauce and stir in 2 tablespoons of the grated cheese. Blend and pour the sauce over the potatoes. Sprinkle with the remaining grated cheese. Bake in moderate oven for 45 minutes.

Lamb, Eggplant and Bean Casserole

Serves 4

4 lamb forequarter chops or 4 middle lamb cutlets
3 tablespoons flour
1 tablespoon curry powder
2 large eggplants
salt
1 tablespoon oil
2 onions
4 carrots
2 sticks celery
125 g haricot beans
3 cups beef stock
1 tablespoon tomato paste

Note If using dried haricot beans, soak overnight beforehand.

Trim any excess fat from the chops. Toss the lamb in the flour seasoned with the curry powder. Shake off any excess. Cut the eggplants into slices 1.5 cm thick. Sprinkle each slice with salt and leave for 30 minutes. Rinse and drain.

Heat oil in pan, add lamb and brown well on both sides. Drain, and transfer meat to casserole dish. Gently fry the peeled and sliced onions, peeled and chopped carrots and sliced celery for 5 minutes and add to the casserole.

Boil the haricot beans for 10 minutes in salted water. Remove the scum from the surface, drain and add to the casserole with the eggplants. Add the tomato paste to the stock and pour over meat and vegetables.

Lamb and Rice Casserole (*See page 28*)

Lamb, Eggplant and Bean Casserole

Cover casserole and bake in moderate oven for 1–1½ hours or until meat and beans are tender. Check seasoning before serving.

Lamb and Rice Casserole

Serves 6

6 lamb chump chops, or middle cutlets
4 tablespoons seasoned flour
2 tablespoons oil
2 tablespoons butter or margarine
2 onions
2 large carrots
1 stalk celery
2 leeks
sprig fresh thyme or ½ teaspoon dried thyme
1 bay leaf
salt and pepper
pinch nutmeg
2 cups water
1 chicken stock cube
1½ cups rice
1 cup peas

Heat the oil and butter in a flameproof casserole dish. Gently fry chopped onions, carrots, celery and sliced leek until tender, stirring from time to time. Remove vegetables and keep warm.

Dredge the chops in the seasoned flour and shallow fry them until well browned on both sides. Return the vegetables to the casserole; add thyme, bay leaf, salt and pepper and nutmeg.

Pour in the water and crumble in the stock cube. Bring to the boil, check the seasoning, then bake in moderate oven for 40 minutes or until meat is tender. Remove casserole from oven and stir in uncooked rice. Bring to the boil on top of the stove, add the peas and cover with a lid. Return casserole to the oven and bake for a further 20 minutes until the rice is tender. If necessary, add extra stock during cooking if the rice absorbs too much liquid.

Lamb Bourguignonne *(See page 35)*

Lamb Jardinière

Serves 6

1 kg boned leg of lamb
1 large onion
1 tablespoon tomato paste
1 beef stock cube
1¼ cups cider
3 cups water
salt and pepper
18 small white onions
250g peas
½ teaspoon sugar
2 tablespoons butter or margarine
250g baby carrots
250g turnips
1 tablespoon oil
2 heaped tablespoons flour

Cut meat into 2.5cm cubes. Heat oil in a pan and brown the lamb for 8 minutes. Place in a casserole. In the same oil fry the peeled and chopped large onion until transparent. Stir in tomato paste and cook for 1 minute. Add cider and water, crumble in stock cube and season. Boil for 10 minutes. Pour the sauce over the meat; cover and simmer for 1½ hours.

Lamb Jardinière

Boil the small onions in salted water until soft; drain. Cook peas in water seasoned with salt and ½ teaspoon sugar. Drain, sprinkle with pepper and toss in 1 tablespoon butter. Boil the carrots, quartered, and turnips cut in strips, separately in salted water. Drain and toss each in remaining butter. Keep all the vegetables warm.

Mix 1 tablespoon oil and the flour over a low heat for 3 or 4 minutes. Add some of the stew gravy, stirring continually until mixture boils; then simmer for 10 minutes. Pour into the casserole and stir over low heat for 5 minutes. Check seasoning.

Pour the stew into the centre of a large serving dish and surround with the vegetables.

Pot Roast Lamb

Serves 8

2 kg leg of lamb, boned, rolled and tied
salt and pepper
2 cloves of garlic
1 tablespoon butter or margarine
1 tablespoon oil
4 carrots
4 parsnips
4 onions
2 cups beef stock
2 cups cooked lima beans
1 tablespoon cornflour

Season the leg of lamb. Lightly cut the skin in several places and insert slivers of garlic. Scrape carrots and parsnips and cut into large pieces. Peel and quarter onions.

Heat butter and oil in a large flameproof dish and brown lamb well on all sides. Remove. Lightly brown carrots, parsnips and onions. Remove. Pour out the fat from the casserole dish and return the lamb. Add stock and bring to boil. Simmer for 1½ hours. Add the vegetables to the meat and simmer further 30 minutes or until meat and vegetables are tender.

Meanwhile heat the lima beans in a little butter and season with salt and pepper. Keep warm.

When the meat and vegetables are cooked remove from casserole and keep warm. Mix the lima beans with the other vegetables.

Skim the fat from the liquid remaining in the casserole dish. Bring to boil and thicken with cornflour mixed with a little cold water. Boil for 5 minutes, strain and check seasoning.

To serve, slice the meat and arrange on a large dish surrounded by the vegetables. Serve the sauce separately.

Oriental Lamb

Serves 6

750 g stewing lamb
seasoned flour
2 tablespoons oil
1 medium onion
2 teaspoons curry powder
1 tablespoon root ginger, grated
pinch cumin
8 black peppercorns
1 tablespoon tomato paste
2 cups water
1 teaspoon treacle
1 bay leaf
2 tablespoons desiccated coconut
1 tablespoon cardamom seeds
2 tomatoes

Cut meat into 2.5 cm cubes and toss in seasoned flour. Heat oil in a pan and brown the meat for 8 minutes, covered with a lid. Remove the meat and keep warm. In the same pan fry the chopped onion until golden brown. Add curry powder, ginger, cumin and crushed peppercorns. Cook for 2 minutes. Stir in the tomato paste and add water, treacle, bay leaf and coconut. Bring to the boil and add the cardamom seeds.

Return meat to the pan and cover with a lid. Reduce heat and simmer for 1½ hours until the meat is tender.

When ready to serve, decorate with the skinned and quartered tomatoes. Serve with boiled rice and a plate of freshly fried poppadoms.

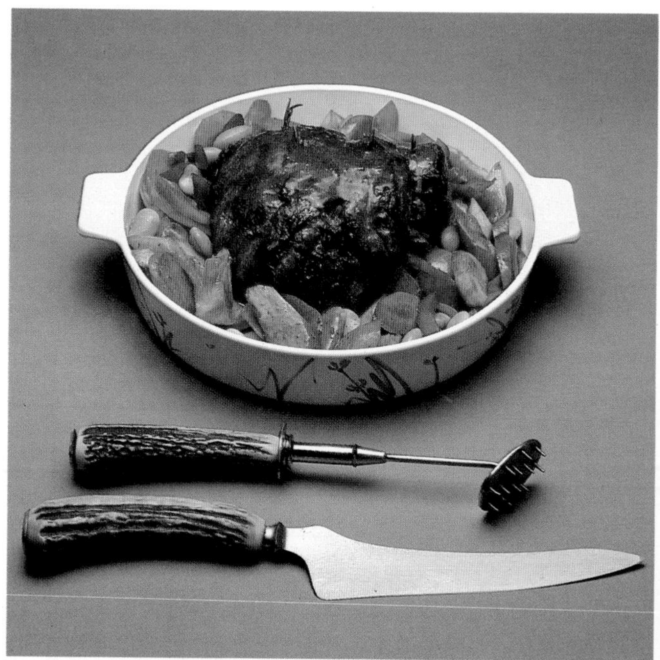

Pot Roast Lamb

Algerian Lamb Casserole

Serves 6

1 kg middle neck cutlets
2 tablespoons oil
500 g onions
500 g potatoes
2½ cups water
½ cup white wine
1 bouquet garni
pinch cumin
salt and pepper
1 bay leaf

Heat oil in a flameproof dish and brown the cutlets on both sides. Add peeled and sliced onions and fry until soft. Add the thinly sliced potatoes, water and wine, bouquet garni, bay leaf, cumin and salt and pepper. Cover casserole and bake in a moderate oven for 1–1½ hours or until the meat and potatoes are tender. Check the seasoning, remove bay leaf and bouquet garni and serve with cooked fennel, celery, carrots or pumpkin.

Lamb Navarin

Serves 4–6

750 g stewing lamb
salt and pepper
1½ tablespoons butter or margarine
1 cup sliced carrots
½ cup sliced onion
2 heaped tablespoons flour
1 tablespoon tomato purée
1 clove garlic

Lamb Navarin

gerian Lamb Casserole

cups beef stock
bouquet garni
)0g new potatoes
tablespoon chopped parsley

im the meat, cut into cubes and season. Heat butter an ovenproof casserole, add the meat and brown ell on all sides. Add carrots and onion and cook til lightly browned. Drain off any surplus fat, add ur and mix. Cook for a few minutes. Add tomato rée and crushed garlic; stir in stock and continue rring until liquid boils and thickens. Simmer for 5 nutes; add bouquet garni. Cover casserole with a l and bake in a moderate oven for 1½ hours.

eanwhile parboil the new potatoes in salted water r 10 minutes.

ter 1½ hours, remove the casserole from the oven d add potatoes. Return to the oven and cook for urther 30 minutes or until meat and potatoes are nder.

move meat and vegetables from casserole and nsfer to a warmed serving dish. Check the asoning of the liquid, skim off fat, and pour over e meat and vegetables. Sprinkle with chopped rsley.

Lancashire Hotpot

Serves 4–6

750g lamb neck or lamb grilling chops
seasoned flour
2 tablespoons oil
4 medium-sized onions
2 lamb's kidneys
250g mushrooms
1 parsnip
750g potatoes
2 cups stock

Trim any excess fat from chops and coat them in seasoned flour. Skin, core and slice kidneys; slice onions, parsnip, potatoes and mushrooms.

Heat oil in pan, add chops and cook for a few minutes until browned on both sides. Remove and drain well.

Arrange the chops, onions, kidneys, mushrooms, parsnip and potatoes in layers in a large casserole, finishing with a layer of potatoes. Pour in stock.

Cover and bake in a moderate oven for 2 hours. Remove the lid and cook for a further 30 minutes to brown the potatoes.

Lamb with Spinach, Egg and Lemon

Serves 4

750g lean lamb, cut in 2 cm cubes
6 tablespoons oil
2 onions, chopped
1 teaspoon salt
freshly ground black pepper
¾ cup beef broth
750g spinach
2 egg yolks
2 tablespoons lemon juice

Heat 4 tablespoons of oil and fry the onions until soft and golden. Add the lamb and fry for 5 minutes over high heat. Add salt, pepper and beef broth, reserving 2 tablespoons of the broth. Simmer gently for 45 minutes or until the meat is tender.

Simmer the cleaned spinach in its own juice in a covered saucepan for 5 minutes until tender. Drain and chop coarsely. Season with salt and pepper. Spread the spinach on top of the meat, drizzle with remaining oil and simmer for 15 minutes.

Beat the egg yolks until creamy and light. Add the lemon juice and reserved beef broth and pour over the meat and spinach. Cook over very low heat for 10 minutes, being careful not to let the mixture boil.

Lamb and Potato Bake

Serves

6 lamb chump chops
25g seasoned flour
50 mL oil
2 onions, sliced
4 tomatoes, peeled, seeded and chopped

Lancashire Hotpot (*See page* 33)

mb and Potato Bake

clove garlic, crushed
0 mL white wine
0 mL chicken stock
bouquet garni
zucchini, sliced
0g potatoes, peeled
0 mL white sauce
g grated cheese

t the oven at 180°C (350°F). Roll the lamb chops in e seasoned flour and brown on both sides in the oil. ansfer to a shallow ovenproof dish. Add the onion the pan and fry until soft. Add the tomatoes, garlic, ne, stock, bouquet garni and seasoning to taste and nmer for 5 minutes.

anch the zucchini in boiling water for 2 minutes and range over the chops. Pour the tomato sauce over e top.

anch the potatoes in boiling water for 5 minutes, ce thinly and arrange over the meat and sauce.

eat the white sauce and stir in 50g of the cheese. ur over the potatoes and sprinkle with the maining cheese. Bake for 45 minutes.

rve immediately, with fresh vegetables.

Lamb Bourguignonne

Serves 6

1 kg boned shoulder of lamb
2 tablespoons oil
3 rashers lean bacon, cut in pieces
2 onions
2 tablespoons tomato paste or purée
1 teaspoon molasses or dark treacle
¾ cup long grain rice
3 tablespoons butter or margarine
6 mushrooms
salt and pepper
pinch mixed spice

Marinade:

1¼ cups dry red wine
¾ cup water
1 bay leaf
2 cloves garlic, crushed
bouquet garni
2 tablespoons vinegar
1 teaspoon sugar

Mix the ingredients for the marinade. Cut the lamb into 2.5 cm cubes and place in a bowl. Pour over the marinade and leave to soak for 3 hours. Lift meat out of the marinade, drain well and dry. Heat oil in a large pan and cook the lamb and bacon pieces for about 6 minutes until browned. Add peeled and chopped onions and sauté for a further 3 minutes. Pour in marinade; add tomato paste, molasses or treacle and bring to boil. Reduce the heat, simmer for 1½ hours.

Meanwhile cook the rice in boiling salted water, drain and stir in half the butter. Sauté the mushrooms in the rest of the butter for 2 minutes.

When the stew has finished cooking, discard bay leaf and bouquet garni. Add mushrooms, check seasoning and add a pinch of mixed spice. Arrange the boiled rice on a heated serving dish and pour the Bourguignonne over it.

Lamb Stew with Pasta

Serves 4

4 lamb chump chops
2 tablespoons oil
1 onion
¼ cup flour
2 tablespoons tomato paste
juice of 2 oranges
1 tablespoon orange peel, cut in thin strips
1¼ cups stock
salt and pepper
2 or 3 zucchini
250 g pasta wheels
1 tablespoon fresh mint, chopped
few mint leaves

Heat oil in a pan and brown chops on both sides. Remove, drain and place in ovenproof dish. Peel and chop onion and fry in pan for 3 minutes; stir in the flour and cook for 1 minute. Add tomato paste and cook for 1 minute. Stir in stock and orange juice and gradually bring to the boil, stirring constantly until mixture thickens. Simmer for further 10 minutes. Season with salt and pepper and pour sauce over chops. Blanch the strips of orange peel in boiling water for 6 minutes; drain and add to meat. Cover casserole and cook in moderate oven for 1 hour.

Meanwhile cut zucchini into large chunks, sprinkle with salt and leave to stand for 30 minutes. Rinse and dry.

Drop pasta into a saucepan of boiling water and keep boiling for 8 minutes. Drain.

Add zucchini and pasta to the stew 15 minutes before the end of cooking time. When ready to serve, check the seasoning, sprinkle with chopped mint and garnish with a few whole mint leaves.

Irish Hotpot

Serves

1 kg stewing lamb
3¾ cups water
salt and pepper
500 g onions
2 leeks
1 kg potatoes
1 tablespoon chopped parsley

Cut meat into even sized pieces. Place in a casserole dish and add the water. Season with salt and pepper and bring to the boil, removing any scum that rises.

Add the peeled and sliced onions, leeks and half the sliced potatoes. Cover and cook in a moderate oven for about 1½ hours. Add the remaining sliced potatoes and cook for a further half hour. If necessar add a little more water.

Sprinkle the hotpot with chopped parsley and serve.

Meatballs in Egg and Lemon Sauce

Serves

1 kg lamb, finely minced
1 onion, finely chopped
1 egg, beaten
½ cup short grain rice
2 tablespoons chopped parsley
2 tablespoons chopped mint, or to taste
½ teaspoon nutmeg
salt and freshly ground pepper to taste
3 cups stock, or water and chicken stock cubes
2 eggs, separated
juice of 1½ lemons

In a large bowl, mix together the meat, onion, egg, rice, parsley, mint and nutmeg, adding salt and pepper to taste. With wet hands, shape the mixture into balls the size of a large walnut. Pour the stock (or water and chicken stock cubes) into a medium-sized saucepan. Quickly bring the stock to boil and add the meatballs. Add salt and pepper to taste. Lower the heat. Cover with a lid and simmer the meatballs over a low heat for 1 hour.

Remove pan from the heat. Whisk egg whites until stiff. Whisk in the egg yolks and lemon juice. Add about a cup of the hot stock to the egg mixture, then pour this into the rest of the stock and meatballs, stirring well as you add. Do not boil after adding egg and lemon mixture. Serve immediately.

Spiced Lamb Lasagne

Serves 6

- 0g lamb, minced
- onion
- tablespoons oil
- teaspoon chilli powder, or to taste
- green pepper
- tablespoon tomato paste
- lt and pepper
- ¾ cup beef stock
- tablespoons raisins
- 85 g lasagne sheets
- cup plain yogurt
- egg
- tablespoon chopped walnuts
- small red pepper

Heat oil in pan and fry the finely chopped onion until softened. Add the minced lamb and stir to brown it evenly. Stir in chilli powder and cook for 1 minute. Add green pepper, seeded and chopped, tomato paste, seasoning, beef stock and raisins. Bring to the boil, cover, and simmer for 40 minutes.

Boil the lasagne sheets in salted water for about 5 minutes or until just tender. Wash the lasagne briskly under cold running water to remove the starch and separate the sheets. Drain and dry sheets on a clean cloth or paper towel.

Spoon a layer of meat sauce into the bottom of an ovenproof dish. Cover with a layer of lasagne. Repeat until the sauce and lasagne are all used, finishing with a layer of sauce on top.

Beat together the yogurt, egg and chopped walnuts. Pour yogurt mixture over the top of the casserole. Arrange the red pepper, seeded and cut into rings, over the yogurt. Place in moderate oven and cook for 20 minutes.

Spiced Lamb Lasagne

PORK

Pork lends itself particularly to salting, smoking and curing and is indeed probably more widely consumed in this form in Australia than it is fresh — hence the inclusion of several recipes calling for ham, gammon or sausages.

Because of pork's high fat content it is advisable to remove as much fat as possible from the dishes before serving. If the dish is not to be served immediately this is simply done by leaving it in the refrigerator for a few hours; the fat will rise to the surface and solidify and can then be easily removed.

Pork Vindaloo (See page 46

Pork Portuguese

Serves 6

1.5 kg lean pork
3 tablespoons flour
salt and pepper
2 tablespoons oil
2 large onions
3 sticks celery
1 green pepper
2 large tomatoes
1¼ cups water
1¼ cups dry white wine
2 tablespoons tomato paste or purée
1 clove garlic
1 bouquet garni
1½ tablespoons cornflour

Cut meat into cubes. Chop onions, coarsely dice celery, seed and dice green pepper, skin and chop tomatoes.

Coat the pork with flour seasoned with salt and pepper. Shake off any excess. Heat the oil in a pan, add the meat, cover and brown for 10 minutes. Transfer to casserole.

In the same pan, gently brown the chopped onions. Add celery, green pepper and tomatoes and sauté for 5 more minutes. Transfer the vegetables to the casserole. Stir in water, wine, tomato paste, crushed garlic and bouquet garni. Season to taste.

Cover casserole and cook in moderate oven for 1½ hours or until meat is tender. Thicken liquid with cornflour mixed with a little cold water. Stir in over a low heat on top of stove.

Serve casserole with a bowl of hot savoury rice.

Pork Portuguese

Salami and Potato Hotpot (*See page* 46)

Pork in Cider

Serves 6

6 pork cutlets
½ cup oil
2 carrots
2 onions
1 clove garlic
2 shallots
1 stick celery
½ cup flour
3 tomatoes
1 cup dry cider or apple juice
bouquet garni
250g canned cream corn
salt and pepper
1 tablespoon chopped parsley

Heat half the oil in a saucepan and gently fry the diced carrots and onions, chopped shallots and thinly sliced celery until tender. Sprinkle in half of the flour, stir and cook for 1 minute. Add skinned and chopped tomatoes and cider. Continue stirring and bring to boil. Add the bouquet garni and corn kernels and season with salt and pepper. Simmer for 15 to 20 minutes.

Coat the cutlets in the remaining seasoned flour and heat the rest of the oil in a pan. Shallow fry the cutlets for about 10 minutes until browned on both sides. Transfer the cutlets to an ovenproof dish. Pour over the sauce and check the seasoning. Cover and bake in a moderate oven for about 30 minutes or until cutlets are tender. Sprinkle with parsley and serve with boiled new potatoes.

Note White wine may be substituted for the cider or apple juice.

Pork Goulash

Serves 6

1.5kg shoulder of pork, cut into 2cm cubes
3 tablespoons butter
4 onions, sliced
1 teaspoon caraway seeds
1 clove garlic, crushed
1 tablespoon chopped fresh dill

Pork Goulash

Pork with Rosemary

or
1 teaspoon dried dill
½ teaspoon salt
freshly ground black pepper
½ cup water
1 tablespoon paprika
1 kg sauerkraut
½ cup sour cream

Heat the butter in a casserole and sauté the onions until golden brown. Stir in the caraway seeds, garlic, dill, salt and pepper. Arrange the pork on top of the onion mixture and pour in the water.

Cover and simmer gently 30 minutes. Check occasionally and add water 1 tablespoon at a time if the mixture is sticking to the pan. Add the paprika and sauerkraut and combine thoroughly.

Cover and cook over very low heat 1 hour or until the pork is tender. Remove from the heat and stir in the sour cream. Serve from the casserole with boiled potatoes.

Pork with Rosemary

Serves 6

1 kg lean boned shoulder or loin of pork in one piece
salt and pepper
125 g butter or margarine
1 carrot
1 large onion
1 stalk celery
375 g mushrooms
1¼ cups water
½ cup dry white wine
2 sprigs rosemary
1 clove garlic

Melt half the butter in a flameproof casserole. Add the seasoned meat and brown on all sides. Remove casserole from the heat. In a separate pan heat the remaining butter. Add the sliced carrot and sauté for 5 minutes. Add chopped onion and diced celery and sauté for a further 5 minutes. Finally add thickly sliced mushrooms, cover pan and cook on a low heat for 2 minutes.

Pour the contents of the pan into the casserole. Add water and wine, one rosemary sprig and crushed garlic. Check the seasoning. Cover casserole and cook in a moderate oven for 1½ hours or until the meat is well cooked.

Serve garnished with the second sprig of rosemary.

Gammon Casserole

Serves 6

750g lean gammon or thick ham steaks
1 tablespoon oil
1 large onion
2 sticks celery
1 cup long grain rice
2 cups chicken stock
250g canned tomatoes, undrained
1 bay leaf
¼ teaspoon each oregano and marjoram
good pinch cinnamon
salt and pepper
125g button mushrooms
250g frozen broad beans

Cut gammon or ham steaks into 2 cm cubes. Heat oil in a pan and fry ham until sealed on all sides. Remove with slotted spoon to a casserole dish.

Add peeled and sliced onion and sliced celery to the pan and fry gently until soft. Add the uncooked rice and stir gently with a fork for 3 minutes. Add the stock, undrained tomatoes, herbs, cinnamon and seasoning. Bring to the boil, pour over the ham and stir well.

Cover casserole and cook in a moderate oven for 1 hour, forking up the rice occasionally. Add more stock if too dry. Add trimmed mushrooms and thawed broad beans and continue to cook for 30 minutes.

Pork in Cider (*See page* 42)

Pork Sausage Casserole

Serves 4

00g pork sausages
tablespoons butter or margarine
onion
apples
cup cider, apple juice, or white wine
chicken stock cube
ouquet garni
inch each mixed spice and cinnamon
alt and pepper
tablespoon tomato paste or purée
2 teaspoons cornflour
¼ cup water

Heat butter in flameproof casserole dish. Fry sausages, sliced onion and peeled, cored and sliced apples until the sausages are browned and onion and apples are soft. Add the cider; crumble in stock cube. Bring to the boil, then add bouquet garni, spices, pepper and salt and tomato paste. Cover casserole dish and bake in moderate oven for about 35 minutes.

Mix cornflour with the water and stir into the casserole on top of the stove, stirring over heat until the liquid thickens.

Serve with baked jacket potatoes topped with chives and sour cream or yogurt. Fried slices of pumpkin and garden peas are also good accompaniments.

Pork Sausage Casserole

Stiermarken Pork Stew

Serves 6

1.25 kg shoulder of pork, cut into 2 cm pieces
3 tablespoons butter
4 onions, coarsely chopped
1 small turnip, cut into strips
4 carrots, cut into strips
1 bay leaf
2 whole cloves
½ teaspoon thyme
½ teaspoon salt
freshly ground black pepper
beef stock or water
1 kg potatoes, peeled and diced
grated fresh horseradish

Heat the butter in a frying pan and sauté the pork over high heat until nicely browned on all sides. With a slotted spoon, transfer the pork to a casserole.

Add the onions, turnip, carrots, bay leaf, cloves, thyme, salt, pepper and enough stock or water to barely cover the ingredients. Bring to a boil, lower the heat and simmer, covered, 1 hour or until the pork is tender.

Cook the potatoes in plenty of boiling salted water 15 to 20 minutes until tender. Remove the bay leaf and cloves. Serve the stew over the diced potatoes and garnish with a generous sprinkling of horseradish.

Salami and Potato Hotpot

Serves 6

2 × 250 g salami sausages
250 g piece of smoked bacon
3 medium onions
3 cloves
bouquet garni
2 bay leaves
1.5 kg small potatoes
1¼ cups dry white wine
salt and pepper

Place the two salami sausages in a pan with the bacon cut into chunks, onions studded with the cloves, bouquet garni, bay leaves and 3¾ cups of water. Bring to the boil and simmer for 40 minutes. Skim off the fat.

Add the peeled potatoes, wine and seasoning to the pan and simmer for a further 30 minutes, or until the potatoes are cooked. Cut salami into chunks to serve.

Pork Vindaloo

Serves 4

500 g spareribs or blade of pork
2 onions
2 cloves garlic
1 red pepper
2 tablespoons oil
2 teaspoons vinegar
1 tablespoon curry powder
2 teaspoons powdered ginger
salt
1 cup water

Cut meat into large chunks or, if using spareribs, remove excess fat and cut ribs in half. Finely chop onions and garlic; seed red pepper and chop. Mix these together with the oil and vinegar and pound to a paste with a pestle and mortar. Stir in curry powder, ginger and a good pinch of salt.

Coat the meat pieces with this mixture and place pork in a large saucepan. Pour in the water, cover, and simmer for 2 hours.

Serve with golden rice — boiled with a pinch of turmeric to colour it.

Oriental Spareribs

Serves 4

1 kg pork spareribs
½ cup vinegar
1¼ cups water
½ cup tomato sauce
6 tablespoons brown sugar
1½ teaspoons soya sauce
salt
2½ tablespoons cornflour
4 tablespoons water

Place spareribs in a baking pan. Combine vinegar and water and pour over meat. Bake in a moderately slow oven for 1 hour. Skim off any fat from the liquid, then strain the liquid into a saucepan.

Stir the combined tomato sauce, brown sugar and soya sauce into the liquid and season with salt to taste. Mix cornflour with the water and add to liquid. Stir over heat to thicken.

Pour the sauce over the drained spareribs and return baking pan to the oven and bake for 30 minutes or until meat is browned. Serve with rice or noodles.

Ham and Apple Casserole

Serves 4

4 thick ham steaks
2 tablespoons butter or margarine
2 onions
2 apples
2 tablespoons flour
1¼ cups dry cider, apple juice, or white wine
½ cup chicken stock
salt and pepper
½ teaspoon dry mustard
250g canned corn kernels, drained
3 tablespoons raisins
125g mushrooms

Melt butter in a pan, fry sliced onions and peeled, cored and sliced apples until soft. Add the ham steaks and brown on both sides. Transfer the ham, onions and apple to a flameproof casserole.

Add the flour to the pan and stir over a low heat for 2 minutes. Add cider and stock and bring to the boil stirring all the time. Simmer and add seasoning, mustard, corn kernels, raisins and sliced mushrooms. Cook for 1 more minute and pour the contents of the pan into the casserole.

Cover casserole and cook in a moderate oven for 45 minutes or until cooked.

Pork Chops with Mushroom Cream Sauce

Serves 4

4 pork chops
2 tablespoons flour
salt and pepper
2 tablespoons butter or margarine
1 large onion
1½ cups sliced mushrooms
1¼ cups cider
¼ cup thickened cream
1 tablespoon chopped parsley

Coat the chops in half the flour seasoned with salt and pepper. Melt butter in a large pan and fry the chops slowly until cooked through. Remove and keep them warm.

Add chopped onion to the pan and fry gently in the meat juices for 3 minutes. Stir in mushrooms and sauté for another 3 minutes. Stir in remaining flour and cook for 1 minute. Take the pan off the heat and gradually stir in the cider to make a smooth sauce. Return pan to heat and stir for 1 minute. Spoon in the cream, stir and season with salt and pepper. Do not allow to boil. Pour sauce over the pork chops, garnish with chopped parsley.

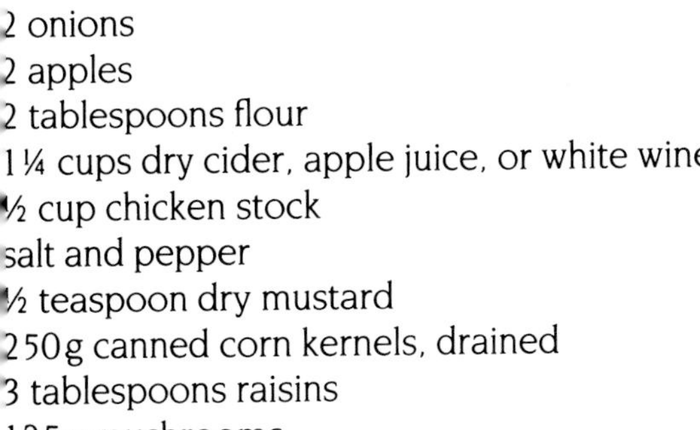

Ham and Apple Casserole

VEAL

White ragoûts of veal — such as Blanquette de Veau, bound with cream or egg yolks — have long been favoured by gourmets. Veal lends itself to such rich, creamy dishes, having greater delicacy of flavour than beef and a much lower fat content than pork or lamb.

The Mediterranean veal dishes such as Osso Buco and Veal Marengo are more tangy and robust in flavour and are particularly good served with rice.

Veal can be used to create tasty and attractive dishes

Blanquette de Veau

Serves 6

1 kg veal shoulder, boned
salt and pepper
2 large carrots
1 large leek
1 stalk of celery
2 cloves garlic
bouquet garni
1 onion studded with 2 cloves
4 tablespoons butter or margarine
2 tablespoons flour
500g small white onions
250g button mushrooms
juice ½ lemon
2 egg yolks
½ cup heavy cream
pinch nutmeg

Trim veal and cut into 3.5 cm cubes. Place in a large saucepan, cover with water and bring to the boil. Drain and rinse in cold water, removing any scum. Return the meat to the saucepan, again cover with water, season with salt and pepper, bring to the boil, then simmer.

Scrape and slice the carrots into 4 pieces, lengthways; trim, clean and chop the leek, chop celery and garlic. Add these, plus the onion studded with cloves and bouquet garni to the meat. Cover and simmer gently for 1¼ hours.

Meanwhile melt 2 tablespoons butter in a small pan, add the flour, blend and cook for 2 minutes and leave to cool. Parboil the small white onions and then fry in 1 tablespoon butter until they are brown and soft. Blanch mushrooms in the remaining butter (1 tablespoon) with the lemon juice and 2 tablespoons water. This liquid may be added to the stew.

When the meat is cooked, remove from pan and keep warm. Remove the carrots, then strain the sauce. Gradually pour about 3½ cups of this liquid into the butter and flour mixture and blend well. Return to heat and continue stirring until the mixture boils and the sauce is thin and smooth. Adjust seasoning.

In another bowl, beat together the egg yolks and cream with a pinch of nutmeg. Stir in about a ½ cup of the unthickened stew liquid, then pour the egg mixture into the thin, hot sauce, stirring briskly until the sauce is thick and smooth.

Return meat, carrots, mushrooms and small onions to a pan and pour the sauce over them. Reheat without bringing to the boil. Place the veal stew in the centre of a heated serving dish and surround with hot noodles or rice.

Braised Veal in Mushroom Sauce

Serves 6

1.25 kg boned leg or shoulder of veal
4 tablespoons butter or margarine
2 shallots
2 onions
1 sprig thyme
1 bay leaf
salt and pepper
1¾ cups of apple cider
250g mushrooms
1 egg yolk
½ cup light cream
2 tablespoons chopped parsley

Heat 3 tablespoons butter in a heavy pan and fry the veal gently until browned on all sides. Lift out. Fry peeled and chopped onions and chopped shallots until softened. Return veal to the pan and add thyme, bay leaf, salt and pepper and cider. Bring to the boil, cover and cook over a low heat for 1½ hours.

Meanwhile sauté the sliced mushrooms in the remaining 1 tablespoon butter heated in a separate pan.

When the veal has been cooking for 1½ hours add the mushrooms and simmer the meat and vegetables for a further 10 minutes.

Drain the veal and place on a serving dish. Keep warm. Discard the thyme and bay leaf. Beat the egg yolk with the cream and beat into the cooking liquid; continue beating until thickened. Pour the sauce over the meat and sprinkle with parsley.

Blanquette de Veau

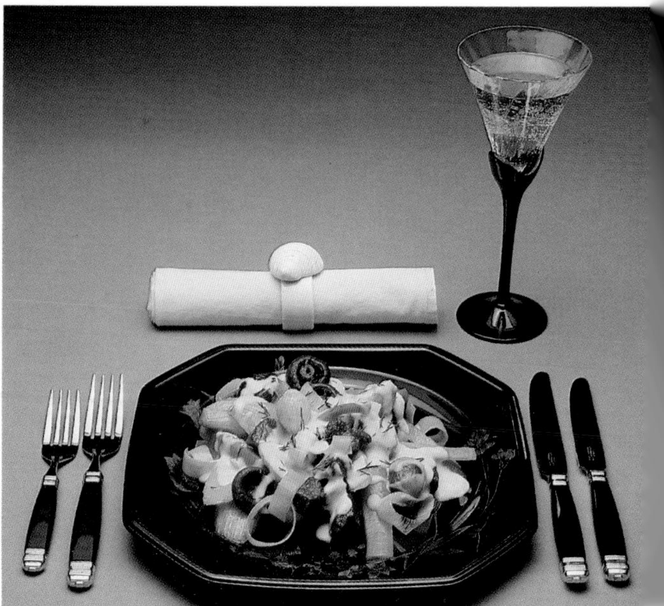

The flavour of mushrooms combines particularly well with vea

Veal with Yogurt

Serves 4

750g boned shoulder of veal
2 tablespoons butter or margarine
2 large onions
1½ cups chicken stock
1 tablespoon paprika
1 tablespoon oil
2 green peppers
4 large tomatoes
1½ cups yogurt

Cut the meat into ½cm slices. Heat butter in a saucepan and fry the veal slices with the peeled and chopped onions until lightly browned. Season with salt and pepper, pour in the stock, add paprika and bring to the boil. Cover and simmer for 20 minutes.

In a separate pan heat the oil, seed and chop the green peppers and fry over a low heat for 10–15 minutes. Then add the skinned and chopped tomatoes and cook for a further 10 minutes, stirring constantly.

Remove the veal and onions from the saucepan and place in a warmed serving dish. Leave the liquid in the pan. Strain the peppers and tomatoes and arrange around the meat. Pour any remaining liquid from them into the liquid from the meat. Stir the yogurt into this combined liquid, return pan to heat and beat for 2 minutes with a whisk. Pour over the veal.

Veal Marengo

Serves 6–8

1 kg boned shoulder veal
½ cup seasoned flour
2 tablespoons oil
2 tablespoons butter or margarine
2 large onions
2 cloves garlic
1¼ cups dry white wine
2 cups water
2 chicken stock cubes
1 tablespoon tomato purée
1 bouquet garni
16 small white onions
250g button mushrooms
2 large tomatoes
1 teaspoon sugar
4 slices white bread
1 tablespoon butter or margarine
2 tablespoons chopped parsley

Cut the veal into 3cm cubes and toss in some of the seasoned flour. Heat half the combined butter and oil in a large pan and fry the meat until brown. Remove and place in casserole dish. Add remaining butter and oil to the frying pan and cook the finely chopped large onions until they are golden brown. Fry the crushed garlic for a minute, then sprinkle in the remaining seasoned flour and stir in until it is just brown. Turn heat off and gradually add the wine and

Veal Marengo

A cream sauce complements many veal dishe

the water in which the stock cubes have been dissolved. Mix well together. Return pan to heat and continue stirring until mixture boils. Add tomato purée and bouquet garni. Simmer gently until the liquid is reduced by about half. Check seasoning and pour over meat. Cook casserole in a moderate oven 1 hour.

Meanwhile peel the small onions and parboil until just soft. Skin and chop tomatoes and slice mushrooms. When the meat is tender, add onions, mushrooms, tomatoes and sugar. Return to oven and cook a further 15 minutes.

Cut the bread into croûtons and fry in the rest of the butter until crisp and golden brown. Dip each croûton into the meat sauce and then in the parsley. Serve the casserole garnished with the croûtons.

Veal Hotpot

Serves 4–5

750g stewing veal
125g bacon pieces
2 tablespoons flour
salt and pepper
2 tablespoons oil
1 large onion
1 green or red pepper
1 clove garlic
2 medium potatoes
1 medium carrot
4 tomatoes
1 tablespoon tomato paste
1 bouquet garni
¼ teaspoon paprika
2 cups water
1 chicken stock cube

Cut the veal into 5cm cubes and dredge in flour seasoned with salt and pepper. Heat the oil in pan and fry the meat until browned. Remove and place in casserole. Lightly fry the bacon pieces, chopped onion and seeded and chopped pepper. Add crushed garlic, peeled and quartered potatoes and carrot and fry for 2 minutes more. Transfer to casserole.

Stir in the tomatoes, skinned and quartered, the tomato paste, bouquet garni and paprika. Boil the water in a saucepan and crumble in the stock cubes; pour over the meat and vegetables. Tightly cover the casserole dish and place in a moderate oven for about 1 hour or until veal is tender.

Veal Ragoût

Serves

750g veal, cut into 2cm cubes
3 tablespoons oil
4 onions, finely chopped
2 cloves garlic, crushed
4 tomatoes, peeled, seeded and chopped
½ cup dry white wine
¼ teaspoon salt
freshly ground black pepper
1½–2 cups chicken stock

Heat the oil in a casserole and sauté the veal until lightly browned. Add the onions and garlic and sauté until brown. Add tomatoes, wine, salt and pepper and simmer 5 minutes. Add the stock and bring to th boil.

Reduce the heat to the lowest possible point and cover the casserole. Place an asbestos pad under the casserole and cook for 2½ to 3 hours. Check from time to time to see if the liquid is evaporating too quickly and add more stock if necessary.

Veal Hotpot

Veal Ragoût

Osso Buco with Artichoke Hearts

Serves 4–6

4 veal shanks or veal knuckles
seasoned flour
2 tablespoons butter
1 large onion
2 cloves garlic
2 carrots
2 stalks celery
½ cup dry white wine
1 cup water
4 large tomatoes
1 tablespoon tomato paste
1 bay leaf
¼ teaspoon dried rosemary
8 canned artichoke hearts
1 lemon
1 tablespoon chopped parsley

Ask butcher to saw veal shanks into 6 cm pieces. Season flour with salt and pepper and roll veal in it. Heat butter in pan and add shanks and brown well on all sides. Remove and place in flameproof casserole dish.

Lightly fry the peeled and sliced onion, crushed garlic, sliced carrots and celery. Add to the meat. Pour wine over meat and vegetables. Stir in skinned and chopped tomatoes, tomato paste, bay leaf, rosemary and water. Bring to boil. Season to taste. Cover and simmer for 1 hour or until meat is tender.

Add drained artichoke hearts and the juice and grated rind of the lemon. Cook for 10 minutes more. Before serving sprinkle on chopped parsley. Serve with boiled potatoes, rice or noodles and a crisp green salad.

Veal Fricassee

Serves 4

750 g stewing veal
2 onions
1 cup dry white wine
1½ cups water
1 bay leaf
¼ teaspoon thyme
salt and pepper
¼ cup flour
2 tablespoons butter
2 tablespoons milk
125 g button mushrooms

Trim the veal, removing any fat and gristle. Cut meat into 3 cm cubes. Place veal pieces, chopped onions, wine and water, herbs and seasoning to taste in a casserole; cover and cook in a moderate oven for about 1¼ hours or until meat is tender. Remove the meat. Strain liquid and reserve.

Make a roux of the flour and butter and cook for 2 minutes. Remove from the heat, add the milk to make a smooth paste, and stir in the reserved liquid to make 1¼ cups of smooth sauce.

Pour the sauce over the veal in a casserole, add sliced mushrooms and return to the oven for 20 minutes. Serve hot.

Veal Mozzarella

Serves 6

750 g veal steaks
juice of 1 lemon
seasoned flour
1 tablespoon oil
30 g butter or margarine
425 g can tomato soup
2 tablespoons dry vermouth
1 teaspoon dried oregano leaves
freshly ground pepper
185 g mozzarella cheese
chopped mint

Veal Fricassee

Osso Buco with Artichoke Heart

Place veal steaks between sheets of plastic wrap and flatten out with a meat mallet. Cut into serving pieces. Put steaks on a plate and pour over lemon juice, leave to stand for at least one hour.

Set oven at 190°C (375°F). Pat veal dry and dust lightly with seasoned flour. Heat oil and butter or margarine in a heavy-based pan and brown veal quickly on both sides. Place veal in a casserole dish, combine tomato soup, vermouth, oregano and pepper and pour over the veal. Place in preheated oven and cook, covered, for 20 minutes.

Slice mozzarella cheese thinly. Remove casserole from oven and place mozzarella cheese on top. Return to the oven uncovered for a further 10 minutes to melt the cheese. Sprinkle with chopped mint to garnish.

Mediterranean Veal Stew

Serves 4

750g shoulder of veal
3 onions
3 tablespoons oil
¼ cup flour
juice of 1 lemon
300 mL chicken stock
2 cloves garlic
500g tomatoes
2 green peppers
250g garden peas
salt and pepper
125g stoned green olives
½ cup light cream

Trim veal and chop into 3 cm cubes. Heat oil in pan and lightly brown the meat pieces and chopped onions. Add the flour and stir while cooking for 2 minutes. Stir in lemon juice, stock, crushed garlic, skinned and chopped tomatoes, seeded and sliced green peppers, garden peas and salt and pepper to taste. Bring to the boil, cover and simmer gently for 25 minutes.

Dip the olives into boiling water for 1 minute, drain and chop them roughly. Add them to the pan and continue to cook for 15 minutes.

Remove the meat and vegetables and transfer to a heated serving dish. Add cream to the pan, check seasoning, and stir over a gentle heat for about 5 minutes. Pour sauce over the meat and serve at once.

Veal Knuckle with Noodles

Serves 4

750g veal knuckle, sawn into 5 cm thick pieces
180g veal kidney
2 tablespoons oil
1 large onion
3 carrots
2 stalks celery
½ cup dry white wine
1 cup chicken stock
1 clove garlic
250g noodles
3 tablespoons butter or margarine
2 tablespoons grated Parmesan cheese
salt and pepper
¼ cup light cream
¼ teaspoon paprika
parsley to garnish

Brown the knuckle pieces and sliced kidney in the oil for 8 minutes. Add peeled and sliced onion and carrots and sliced celery. Cover and simmer very gently for 10 minutes. Transfer to casserole dish. Pour in the combined stock and wine, add the crushed garlic and season to taste. Cover, place in a moderate oven and cook for 1½–2 hours or until meat is tender. Remove from oven and stir in the cream and paprika. Reheat on top of the stove.

Boil noodles in salted water for 8–10 minutes until tender. Drain them and stir in butter, Parmesan cheese and salt and pepper to taste.

Arrange noodles around a heated serving dish and fill centre with the meat and sauce. Garnish with sprigs of parsley and serve at once.

Mediterranean Veal Stew

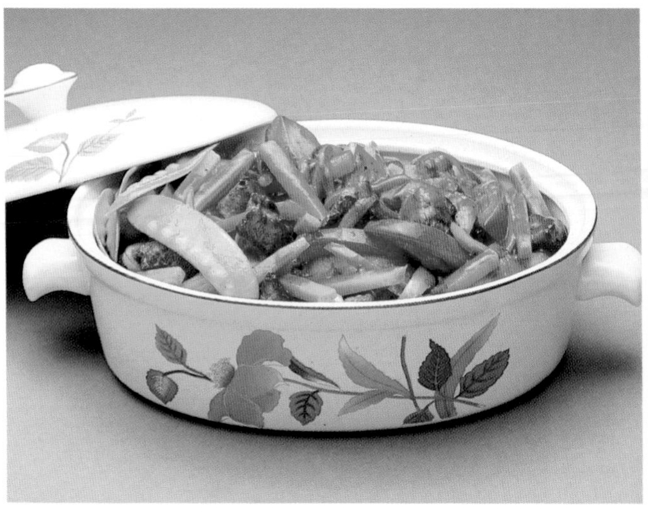

Veal Knuckle with Noodles is an ideal luncheon dish

CHICKEN AND GAME

Chicken pieces are now widely available and cheap to buy and make an excellent foundation for most of the dishes in this chapter. Some, such as Coq au Vin and Chicken in Port, are rich and festive; others are simpler — perfect for everyday family meals. Cooking time need not be long since chicken meat is generally quite tender and will become dry and stringy if overcooked.

Game birds and rabbit have full, distinctive flavours and make unusual and delicious meals. They are readily available at specialist poultry shops and some delicatessens.

Farmhouse Chicken and Potato Casserole (See page 62)

Farmhouse Chicken and Potato Casserole

Serves 4

4 chicken pieces
cornflour
salt and pepper
2 tablespoons butter or margarine
1 tablespoon oil
500g potatoes
4 lean bacon rashers
60g mushrooms
8 small white onions
¾ cup chicken stock
1 tablespoon chopped chives

Season cornflour with salt and pepper and roll chicken pieces in it. Heat butter and oil in a pan and fry the chicken pieces until they are brown on both sides. Remove chicken, drain, and place in an ovenproof casserole with the peeled and quartered potatoes.

Remove rind from bacon and cut into strips, slice mushrooms, peel the small onions, and add to the pan, frying until golden. Transfer to the casserole. Pour the stock into the pan and stir to incorporate all the pan juices. Bring to the boil, then pour the stock into the casserole. Cover the dish and bake in a moderate oven for 1 hour or until chicken is tender.

Check seasoning and sprinkle the finished dish with chopped chives.

Chicken in Port

Serves 6

1 × 1.5kg chicken
3 tablespoons flour
salt and pepper
¼ cup oil
1 onion
125g lean bacon
125g button mushrooms
1 cup port
¾ cup sour cream or yogurt
½ teaspoon honey

Chicken in Port

Poulet Lavandou (*See page 64*)

Cut chicken into 8 pieces. Coat each with seasoned flour and shake off any excess. Heat oil in a large pan and add chicken pieces, frying gently for 10 minutes and turning occasionally so that they brown on all sides. Transfer chicken to a flameproof casserole.

In the same oil fry the chopped onion and bacon pieces for 2 minutes. Add sliced mushrooms and cook for 1 more minute. Stir in the port, season and simmer for 5 minutes. Pour this sauce over the chicken, cover casserole dish and place in moderate oven for 25 minutes, or until chicken is tender.

Blend the sour cream or yogurt and honey in a bowl. Remove the casserole from the oven and transfer chicken pieces to a warmed serving dish. Add the cream mixture to the sauce and cook on top of the stove for 1 minute over a low heat, stirring continually. Pour the sauce over the chicken pieces and serve immediately.

Poulet Lavandou

Serves 4

4 chicken pieces
2 tablespoons butter or margarine
125g smoked bacon
1 onion
4 shallots
1 carrot
1 tablespoon flour
1¼ cups dry white wine
3 tablespoons tomato paste
¼ teaspoon fennel seeds
salt and pepper
1 tablespoon butter, extra
250g mushrooms
125g green olives

Melt the 2 tablespoons butter in a large pan, add the bacon cut into strips, and fry until lightly browned. Remove from the pan with a slotted spoon and drain on absorbent paper. Add chicken pieces to the pan and fry until golden. Remove and drain on absorbent paper.

Fry peeled and finely chopped onion, shallots and carrot for 5 minutes; stir in the flour and cook for 2 minutes. Gradually add the combined wine and tomato paste, stirring continuously until mixture boils. Stir in fennel seeds, add seasoning and simmer gently for 15 minutes. Return chicken pieces to the pan, cover and simmer for a further 30 minutes or until chicken is tender.

Meanwhile heat 1 tablespoon butter in small pan and fry the washed and sliced mushrooms for 3 or 4 minutes. If using button mushrooms leave whole. Remove from the pan and drain. Remove stones from the olives and place the olives in a saucepan with just enough cold water to cover. Bring to boil and simmer for 5 minutes. Drain and rinse in cold water.

When the chicken is tender remove from the pan and liquidise or sieve the sauce. Return sauce to pan with the chicken, bacon, mushrooms and olives and cook gently for 10 minutes to heat through.

Transfer to a heated serving dish and serve piping hot with creamed potatoes and a green vegetable.

Chicken and Mushrooms

Chicken and mushrooms

Serves 4–6

1 × 1.5kg roasting chicken
2 tablespoons flour
salt and pepper
2 tablespoons oil
4 shallots
125g button mushrooms
½ cup white vermouth, dry sherry or white madeira
1¼ cups chicken stock
1 teaspoon tomato paste or purée
1 teaspoon chopped parsley
1 bay leaf

Chicken dishes are always popular for entertaining

Cut the chicken into serving pieces. Season the flour with the salt and pepper and roll the chicken pieces in it. Heat the oil in a large pan and fry chicken until each piece is well browned. Add sliced shallots and whole button mushrooms and sauté for about 5 minutes.

Transfer the chicken mixture to a casserole dish, pour over the vermouth and chicken stock and add tomato paste, parsley and bay leaf. Adjust the seasoning. Cover and cook in a moderate oven for 1 hour. Before serving remove the bay leaf.

Poulet à Deux

Serves 2

250g cooked chicken
1 red pepper
1 green pepper
50g butter
50g button mushrooms, sliced
40g flour
150 mL hot chicken stock
50 mL milk
50 mL single cream
150 mL white wine
1 tablespoon brandy

Cut the red and green pepper into small cubes and blanch in boiling water for 2 minutes. Drain well. Cut the chicken into small cubes.

Melt the butter in a frying pan. Add the mushrooms and fry gently for 2–3 minutes. Stir in the flour and cook for 2 minutes, stirring. Gradually add the hot stock, bring to the boil and simmer for 2–3 minutes. Stir in the milk and cream and season to taste.

Stir in the wine and brandy, add the red and green peppers and the chicken and heat through gently.

Serve immediately, with boiled rice.

Poulet à Deux

Apricot Chicken

Serves 4–6

1 × 1.5kg chicken
250g apricots or 125g dried apricots
2 medium onions, chopped finely
2 medium tomatoes, chopped roughly
2 cloves garlic
½ teaspoon ginger
¼ teaspoon chilli powder
¼ teaspoon saffron
1 tablespoon hot milk
1 tablespoon ghee or oil
¼ teaspoon garam marsala
2 teaspoons salt
3 cups warm water

Joint the chicken into pieces. Stone apricots. (If using dried apricots, soak in water overnight.) Pound garlic into a paste with the ginger and chilli. Crumble the saffron into the hot milk and let it dissolve.

In a saucepan heat the ghee and fry the onions until pale golden. Put in the garlic, ginger and chilli paste and fry with the onions 5 minutes, stirring often.

Now add the chicken pieces, garam marsala, tomatoes and salt to the pan. Pour in warm water, cover and simmer gently until chicken is cooked and tender. Remove cover now and add a little warm water if liquid has evaporated.

When chicken is tender, add the saffron milk and apricots and cook gently until apricots are soft and tender. Serve hot.

Note Duck or any other poultry can be used with peaches or apricots. Tinned fruit can be used, but drain the syrup.

:oq au Vin

Serves 6

:g chicken pieces
tablespoons flour
lt and pepper
tablespoons butter or margarine
!5 g salt pork or bacon rashers
small carrots
! tiny white onions
tablespoon butter or margarine, extra
cup brandy
tomatoes
1 clove garlic
1½ cups red wine
1 tablespoon chopped parsley
½ teaspoon dried thyme
1 bay leaf
salt and pepper
250g button mushrooms

Wash and dry the chicken pieces and toss in flour seasoned with salt and pepper. Cut the pork or bacon rashers into strips. Peel and slice carrots, peel onions, skin, seed and chop tomatoes.

Heat butter in a heavy flameproof saucepan and fry the pork or bacon strips until lightly browned. Add

\pricot Chicken

the carrots and whole onions and fry until golden brown. Remove with a slotted spoon and drain on absorbent paper.

Add the extra tablespoon of butter to the pan, heat and fry the chicken pieces until browned on all sides. Warm the brandy, pour over the chicken and set alight. When finished flaming, add tomatoes and crushed garlic and cook for a few minutes. Return the pork or bacon slices, onions and carrots to the pan. Pour in red wine, add parsley, thyme and bay leaf and bring to the boil, stirring continuously. Add salt and pepper to taste, then cover and simmer over low heat for 45 minutes.

Wipe the mushrooms, trim the stalks and add to the casserole. Continue cooking a further 15 minutes or until chicken is tender.

Remove the bay leaf, taste and adjust seasoning. Serve hot straight from the casserole.

Chicken and Vegetable Stew

Serves 4–6

1.5 kg chicken pieces
1 teaspoon salt
black pepper to taste
¼ teaspoon marjoram
½ teaspoon paprika
3 tablespoons butter
2 tablespoons oil
2 large onions
2 large carrots
1 leek
500 g canned butter beans
1¼ cups chicken stock
1 teaspoon lemon juice

Thoroughly dry chicken pieces and rub with the combined salt, pepper, marjoram and paprika. Heat 2 tablespoons butter and 1 tablespoon oil in a pan and fry chicken pieces for about 10 minutes, turning every so often so they will be evenly browned.

Peel onions and cut into rings; peel and slice carrots. Remove green part of the leek, wash and cut remainder into rings. Drain the butter beans.

Heat remaining 1 tablespoon butter and 1 tablespoon oil in a large clean, heavy pan. Add onion slices and fry until golden brown. Add carrots, leeks and beans and cook over a low heat for 15 minutes. Add the drained chicken pieces and the chicken stock. Cover tightly and simmer for 1 hour or until tender.

Taste for seasoning and adjust if necessary. Add lemon juice and serve.

Chicken Tarragon

Serves

1 × 1.5 kg chicken
1 tablespoon butter
½ teaspoon salt
freshly ground black pepper
1 teaspoon dried tarragon
2 tablespoons butter
2 carrots, diced
1 medium sized onion, finely chopped
½ cup chicken stock
½ teaspoon dried tarragon
1 tablespoon cornflour dissolved in 2 tablespoons water

Place the 1 tablespoon of butter in the cavity of the chicken. Sprinkle in the salt, pepper and tarragon and truss the chicken. Heat 2 tablespoons of butter in a heavy casserole until foaming and brown the chicken on all sides. Remove it from the pan and set aside.

If the butter is too brown, discard it and melt another 2 tablespoons of butter in the casserole. Add the carrots and onion and cook until softened. Replace the chicken in the casserole on the bed of vegetables. Add the stock and ½ teaspoon of tarragon. Cover with aluminium foil, then a lid and simmer slowly on top of the stove or in a 180°C (350°F) oven for 50 minutes or until chicken is tender.

Cut the chicken into serving pieces and place on a warmed platter. Thicken the pan juices with the cornflour mixture. Pour the sauce with the vegetables over the chicken and serve hot.

Chicken Juliet

Serves 4–

1 × 1.5 kg chicken
seasoned flour
2 tablespoons butter or margarine
2 tablespoons oil
1 large onion
2 cups chicken stock
½ cup dry white wine
1 tablespoon Worcestershire sauce
1½ tablespoons flour, extra
1 orange
⅓ cup sultanas

Cut chicken into serving pieces and toss in seasoned flour. Heat butter and oil in large pan, add chicken pieces and brown well on all sides. Remove from pan drain on absorbent paper and place pieces in ovenproof casserole dish.

Add peeled and thickly sliced onion to pan. Cook gently until soft but not browned. Remove, drain, and place in casserole.

Add extra flour to pan, stir until combined and cook 1 minute. Remove from heat. Stir in chicken stock, wine, juice of the orange and Worcestershire sauce. Return pan to heat and stir until mixture boils and thickens. Add sultanas and thinly pared orange rind cut into strips. Pour sauce over chicken and onions.

Cover the casserole and cook in a moderate oven for 1 hour or until chicken is tender.

Duck Italian Style

Serves 8

2 × 1.5 kg ducks
60 g butter
¼ cup oil
2 large onions, chopped
2 carrots, sliced
2 stalks celery, chopped
125 g bacon pieces
1 kg tomatoes
1¼ cups chicken stock
½ cup dry white wine
¼ teaspoon combined basil and sage
1 teaspoon chopped parsley
salt and pepper
375 g ribbon pasta
⅓ cup grated Parmesan cheese
2 teaspoons cornflour

Cut each duck into 4 pieces. Heat half the butter and all the oil in a large pan and add the duck pieces. Cover and brown on all sides for 10 minutes. Remove, drain, and transfer the duck to a large flameproof casserole.

Add the onions to the pan and sauté gently until transparent. Add the carrots and celery and stir-fry for a further 5 minutes until lightly browned. Transfer all the vegetables to casserole and discard the fats in the pan.

Add the bacon pieces, skinned and chopped tomatoes, chicken stock and wine to the casserole. Stir in the herbs and season to taste. Cover and cook the casserole slowly over a gentle heat for 45–60 minutes or until the duck is tender. Remove the duck pieces and strain the casserole liquids into a clean pan. Keep the duck warm in the oven.

Duck Italian Style

Meanwhile boil the ribbon pasta in salted water for 10 minutes or until tender. Drain and transfer to a large ovenproof serving dish. Toss the pasta in the remaining butter with the cheese and arrange the duck on top. Keep warm.

Skim off any fat that may have formed on the top of the casserole juices. Mix the cornflour with a ¼ cup of warm water. Heat the casserole juices and stir in the cornflour paste, stirring over a gentle heat, until the gravy is smooth. Pour some of this gravy over the duck and pasta and serve the rest in a gravy boat. Return the duck and pasta to the oven for 5 minutes to allow the gravy to soak through the pasta.

Serve with a green vegetable of your choice and a crisp tossed green salad.

Turkey Bonne Femme

Serves 4

4 turkey portions
125g bacon rashers
2 carrots
2 onions
4 leeks
1 stalk celery
90g butter or margarine
1 bouquet garni
salt and pepper
1 cup chicken stock
250g mushrooms
juice of 2 lemons
4 medium potatoes
1 egg yolk
½ cup cream

Skin the turkey pieces; derind and cut the bacon rashers into small strips and blanch by putting the bacon pieces in a saucepan with just enough water to cover. Bring to the boil, then simmer gently for 5 minutes, drain and rinse with cold water. Meanwhile peel and slice the carrots and onions; wash and chop the white parts of the leeks finely and slice the celery.

Melt 30g of the butter in a large flameproof casserole, add the prepared vegetables, bacon and the bouquet garni. Fry gently for 10 minutes, stirring occasionally. Add the turkey portions, sprinkle with salt and pepper, then pour in the chicken stock. Cover the casserole tightly and cook over a low heat for 1 hour. Check the liquid occasionally and add more stock if necessary.

Meanwhile trim the stalks of the mushrooms and slice. If using button mushrooms, leave whole. Melt the remaining butter (30g) in a saucepan, add half the lemon juice, then the mushrooms. Add salt and pepper to taste and enough water to just cover. Simmer gently until mushrooms are soft. Remove from heat and set aside.

Peel the potatoes and add to the turkey when it has been cooking for 1 hour; cook for a further 30 minutes.

Put the egg yolk and remaining lemon juice in a bowl and beat in the cream with 1 or 2 tablespoons of the hot sauce.

Drain the turkey and potatoes and arrange in a warmed serving dish. Remove the bouquet garni from the sauce, then gradually stir in the egg yolk mixture. Heat gently, stirring constantly, then add mushrooms and heat through for a minute or two. Taste and adjust the seasoning and pour the sauce over the turkey and potatoes.

Pheasant Casserole

Serves 6

1 × 1.25kg pheasant
¼ cup flour
salt and pepper
¼ cup oil
1 onion, sliced
60g sliced mushrooms
1 red and 1 green pepper
½ cup red wine
1¼ cups of stock made with 2 chicken stock cubes
1 tablespoon tomato paste or purée
salt and pepper
pinch ground mace
1 tablespoon cornflour
⅓ cup water

Cut the pheasant into 6 serving pieces: drumsticks, thighs and breasts. Coat pieces with flour seasoned with salt and pepper. Heat oil in a pan and fry pheasant pieces until golden brown on all sides. Remove, drain, and transfer to casserole dish.

In the same oil fry onion slices until transparent. Add seeded and diced green and red peppers and sliced mushrooms and sauté for a few minutes. Pour in wine, bring to the boil and simmer gently for 5 minutes. Add the stock, tomato paste, seasoning and mace to the pan. Bring to the boil, then reduce the heat. Mix the cornflour in the ⅓ cup of water and add to the pan, stirring until the mixture boils and thickens. Pour over the pieces of pheasant in the casserole, cover, and cook in a moderate oven for 45–60 minutes or until the pheasant is very tender.

Transfer meat and sauce to a heated serving dish and serve with creamed potatoes.

Pheasant Casserole

Rabbit with Mustard

Serves 4

1 young (1.25–1.5 kg) rabbit or substitute chicken
4 tablespoons mild French mustard
1 teaspoon salt
freshly ground black pepper
6 thin slices bacon
½ cup cream
1 tablespoon flour *combined with* 2 tablespoons cream

Spread 2 tablespoons of the mustard in the cavity of the rabbit. Sprinkle the outside with salt and pepper. Cover the rabbit with bacon slices and spread the bacon with the remaining mustard. Place the rabbit in a heavy casserole just large enough to hold it. Cover and cook in a 180°C (350°F) oven for 1 to 1½ hours or until tender.

Transfer the rabbit to a heated platter. Add cream to the pan juices and bring to a simmer. Stir in the flour and cream mixture with a wire whisk and cook, stirring, 2 to 3 minutes. Cover the rabbit with a little of the sauce and pass the rest separately. This dish is equally good using chicken so don't hesitate to try it.

Rabbit Romain

Serves 4

1 rabbit
½ cup flour
salt and pepper
125g bacon
60g butter or margarine
2 medium onions, sliced
1 clove garlic, chopped
2 carrots, sliced
½ cup dry white wine
½ cup chicken stock
2 sprigs thyme
2 sprigs rosemary

Cut the rabbit into joints and coat in flour seasoned with salt and pepper. Cut the bacon into chunks and fry in the butter for 5 minutes. Remove and place in a large earthenware casserole. Fry the rabbit joints until they are lightly browned on all sides and transfer them to the casserole.

Fry the sliced onions until golden and add the chopped garlic and cook for a further minute. Sauté the sliced carrots lightly, stirring. Add the white wine and the chicken stock to the frypan, season with salt and pepper and bring to the boil, stirring continually. Pour the mixture over the meat and add sprigs of thyme and rosemary. Cover the casserole and cook in a moderate oven for 1–1½ hours or until rabbit is tender. At this stage the sauce may be thickened wit a little cornflour dissolved in water and stirred over a low heat on top of the stove. A few tablespoons of cream stirred into the sauce before serving will add to the smooth, rich flavour.

Rabbit Bourguignonne

Serves 6-

8 rabbit portions
2 to 3 tablespoons seasoned flour
3 tablespoons butter or margarine
125g lean bacon rashers
2 large onions
¼ cup of brandy
1¾ cups dry white wine
1 bouquet garni
1 teaspoon sugar
2 cloves garlic
¼ teaspoon each tarragon and chervil
1 sprig parsley
24 button onions
250g mushrooms
1 tablespoon oil
1 teaspoon Dijon mustard
½ cup heavy cream
1 tablespoon chopped parsley

Dredge the rabbit pieces with seasoned flour. Heat butter in flameproof casserole dish and brown the rabbit on both sides. Cook for about 10 minutes. Add chopped bacon and fry for 2 minutes, then add peeled and chopped onions and cook for 2 more minutes. Warm the brandy, pour into casserole and set alight. Add the white wine to extinguish the flames, then add bouquet garni, sugar, crushed garlic and herbs. Season, bring to the boil, cover with a lid and simmer for 40 minutes.

Meanwhile boil the peeled button onions in salted water for 5 minutes and strain. Fry the sliced mushrooms in the oil, and drain. When the rabbit is tender add onions and mushrooms. Remove the bouquet garni.

In a separate bowl mix the mustard and cream together and stir in about 5 tablespoons of the rabbit cooking liquid and blend well. Pour this back into the casserole and heat through, stirring constantly. Do not allow to boil.

Sprinkle with chopped parsley and serve with boiled new potatoes and a green salad.

Rabbit Bourguignonne

FISH

This chapter features some good ideas for cooking with fish which provide a welcome change from the traditional fried fish-and-chips dinner. Fish such as bream, flake and gemfish are usually plentiful and cheap and make a delicious combination with vegetables, spices and stock.

Trout in Red Wine is an excellent dinner party or special occasion dish. For convenience try Tuna and Macaroni Casserole; the recipe calls for canned tuna and makes a quick and easy family meal that is particularly popular with children.

Burgundian Fish Stew (*See page* 76)

750 ml
14 LB
TO WEIGH
STEVENS & SON

Burgundian Fish Stew

Serves 6

1.5kg mixed fish
3 tablespoons butter
3 tablespoons olive oil
1 large bacon rasher, chopped
3 tablespoons plain flour
2 cups dry white wine
4 cups water
1 clove garlic, crushed
1 bay leaf
¼ teaspoon ground thyme
⅛ teaspoon ground nutmeg
2 tablespoons chopped parsley
salt and pepper
½ cup cognac or brandy
toasted French bread

Heat butter and oil in a flameproof casserole, brown bacon, add flour and cook, stirring, until browned. Gradually stir in wine and water. Bring to the boil. Add garlic, bay leaf, thyme, nutmeg, parsley and seasoning. Cover and cook gently for 20 minutes. Add fish cut into serving pieces and cook, covered, for another 10 minutes.

Warm cognac, set alight, pour into casserole, shake gently until flames die down. Arrange toast around the edge. Serve in soup bowls.

Bream and Mushroom Casserole

Serves

750g bream fillets
2 shallots
1 tablespoon butter or margarine
250g button mushrooms, sliced
1 egg yolk
½ cup heavy cream
1 teaspoon cornflour
juice ½ lemon
1 teaspoon chopped parsley
1 coriander leaf (optional)

Stock:

1 small chopped onion
2 tablespoons butter or margarine
250g fish bones
2½ cups dry white wine
bouquet garni
salt and pepper

To make the stock: Fry onions in the butter for about 4 minutes, add fish bones, wine, bouquet garni and seasoning. Boil for 5 minutes, then strain and reserve the liquid.

Bream and Mushroom Casserole

Haddock Risotto (See page 78)

BIANCO
Castel Giunti
RICCARDO GIUNTI & FIGLI
POGGIBONSI - TOSCANA
PRODUTTRICE VINICOLA
ALCOOL GRADI 12
OIL

Grease a casserole dish, sprinkle in the chopped shallots and arrange seasoned fish fillets on top. Add half the sliced mushrooms and pour in the stock. Cover and bake in a moderate oven for 20 minutes. Remove the fish fillets and place on a serving dish.

Combine the egg yolk, cream and cornflour. Place the casserole dish containing the stock over a low heat on top of the stove and gradually add the cream and egg mixture, stirring continually. Check seasoning, then add lemon juice.

Sauté the remaining sliced mushrooms in 1 tablespoon butter and then toss in the chopped parsley. Pour the thickened sauce over the fish and garnish with the sautéed mushrooms and coriander leaf.

Haddock Risotto

Serves 4

500g smoked haddock or cod
¼ cup oil
1 large onion
1 clove garlic
1 large green pepper
3 large tomatoes
125g button mushrooms, quartered
½ cup long grain rice
salt and pepper
1¼ cups chicken stock
juice ½ lemon
2 tablespoons butter or margarine
¼ teaspoon paprika

Poach fish in water for a few minutes until tender but not mushy. Drain and flake into pieces.

Heat the oil in a deep flameproof pan. Peel and slice the onion and fry for 3 minutes. Add peeled and chopped garlic and the seeded and sliced green pepper and fry for another 3 minutes. Stir in mushroom pieces and cook a further 1 minute, then add the skinned and chopped tomatoes. Stir in rice and cook until it has absorbed the vegetable juices. Season with salt and pepper. Pour in the stock and bring to the boil. Cover and simmer very gently for 20 minutes until the rice is tender, checking from time to time that there is enough liquid to prevent the rice from sticking — add a little water if necessary.

When the rice is cooked, remove the pan from the heat. Add the lemon juice and gently stir in the haddock pieces. Transfer to a heated serving dish, stir in the butter to melt, and dust with the paprika. Serve at once.

Fisherman's Stew

Serves

2 kg of varied fish (whiting, gemfish, bream)
salt, pepper
1 large onion, finely chopped
3 shallots, sliced
1 leek (white part only), sliced
2 or 3 stalks of celery, sliced
1 bouquet garni
4 cups of red or white wine
4 tablespoons butter or margarine
3 or 4 bacon rashers
250g button mushrooms
12 small onions
4 tablespoons flour

Garnish:

6 slices of bread
½ cup oil
1 tablespoon chopped parsley

Clean, scale and wash fish, and cut them across bone into thick steaks. Place the fish pieces in flameproof casserole, season with salt and pepper. Add sliced onion, shallots, leek, celery, bouquet garni and wine. Bring to the boil, reduce heat and simmer for 15–20 minutes.

Meanwhile heat 1 tablespoon butter in a pan, add diced bacon and sauté for 3 or 4 minutes. Remove bacon and keep warm. To the same pan add mushrooms and sauté gently for 3 minutes. Drain and keep warm.

Add extra tablespoon of butter and cook whole onions until softened and lightly browned. Drain.

When the fish is cooked lift out with a slotted spoon and place the pieces on a serving dish. Add the drained bacon, mushrooms and onions. Keep warm while thickening stock.

Heat two tablespoons butter in pan and stir in the flour. Cook, stirring, until flour is lightly golden. Gradually add the strained stock in which fish has been cooked. Stir until sauce boils. Check seasoning. Reduce heat and simmer for 5 minutes. Pour thickened sauce over fish mixture.

Garnish: Remove crusts from bread and cut into triangular pieces. Heat oil in clean pan and fry bread until golden brown on both sides. Drain. Dip the points of bread pieces into the sauce and then in chopped parsley. Arrange around the dish.

Fisherman's Stew

Hamburg Fish Casserole

Serves 6

1 × 500g package frozen fish fillets, cut into bite-size pieces
2 tablespoons margarine or butter
1 medium onion, chopped
250g scallops
250g prawns, shelled and cleaned
1 can artichoke hearts, drained
1 small can sliced mushrooms, drained
1 can mushroom soup
1 cup dry white wine
½ teaspoon salt
2 cups cooked rice
2 teaspoons chopped parsley
2 tablespoons grated Parmesan cheese

Melt margarine in large skillet; sauté onion until transparent. Add fish, scallops, prawns, artichoke hearts, mushrooms, soup, wine and salt; mix well.

Combine rice and parsley in large greased casserole. Pour fish mixture over rice. Bake in a moderate oven 170°C (350°F) for 20 minutes. Sprinkle cheese over top; bake 10 minutes longer.

Tuna and Macaroni Casserole

Serves 4–5

220g can chunk-style tuna
1 cup macaroni
2 tablespoons butter or margarine
1 large onion
2 tablespoons flour
1 tablespoon dry mustard
3 cups milk
salt and pepper
1 tablespoon Worcestershire sauce
135g tasty cheese, grated

Topping:

strips of cheese
2 small tomatoes
pinch sugar
salt and pepper

Heat butter in a saucepan and add the chopped onion and sauté until soft. Stir in flour and dry mustard, combine, and cook for a few minutes. Remove pan from heat and stir in half the milk and mix until smooth. Return pan to heat and gradually add the remaining milk, stirring continually until the sauce boils and thickens. Season to taste; add the Worcestershire sauce and grated cheese. Stir and simmer gently for 5 minutes or until cheese has melted. Mix in the drained tuna.

Combine the fish mixture with the cooked macaroni and spoon into greased casserole dish. Top with narrow strips of cheese, placed lengthways and across to form a pattern of squares. Place a slice of tomato in each square, sprinkle tomato slices with a few grains of sugar and a sprinkle of salt and pepper. Place in a moderate oven for 30 minutes and serve direct from casserole.

German Fish Stew

Serves 6–

2 × 500g packages frozen fish fillets, cut into serving size pieces
4 medium onions, sliced
1 stalk celery, chopped
1 tablespoon salt
2 tablespoons margarine or butter
5 cups milk
½ cup sour cream
2 tablespoons chopped dill pickle
4 teaspoons horseradish
1 teaspoon parsley flakes
fresh chopped dill

Place onions, celery, fish, salt and margarine in large heavy saucepan; add milk. Bring to a boil; reduce heat; simmer 15–20 minutes. Add sour cream, pickle, horseradish and parsley; stir to blend; heat. Garnish with dill.

Oslo Fish Stew

Serves

250g fresh or frozen cod fillets
6 potatoes
3 onions
6 tomatoes
2 red peppers
1 large cucumber
1 clove garlic
1 teaspoon salt
black pepper to taste
½ cup cooking oil

using fresh fish place in a little cold water and poach ently. Frozen cod should be thawed first.

ut the fish fillets across in thick slices. Peel and slice otatoes, peel and cut onions into wedges, skin, seed nd cut tomatoes into quarters, seed and cut red eppers into strips, peel and cut cucumber into thick unks.

Layer the fish and the vegetables with the crushed garlic in an ovenproof casserole. Season and pour in the oil. Cover with a lid and place in a moderately hot oven for about 45 minutes or until the vegetables are cooked.

Serve straight from the casserole.

Oslo Fish Stew

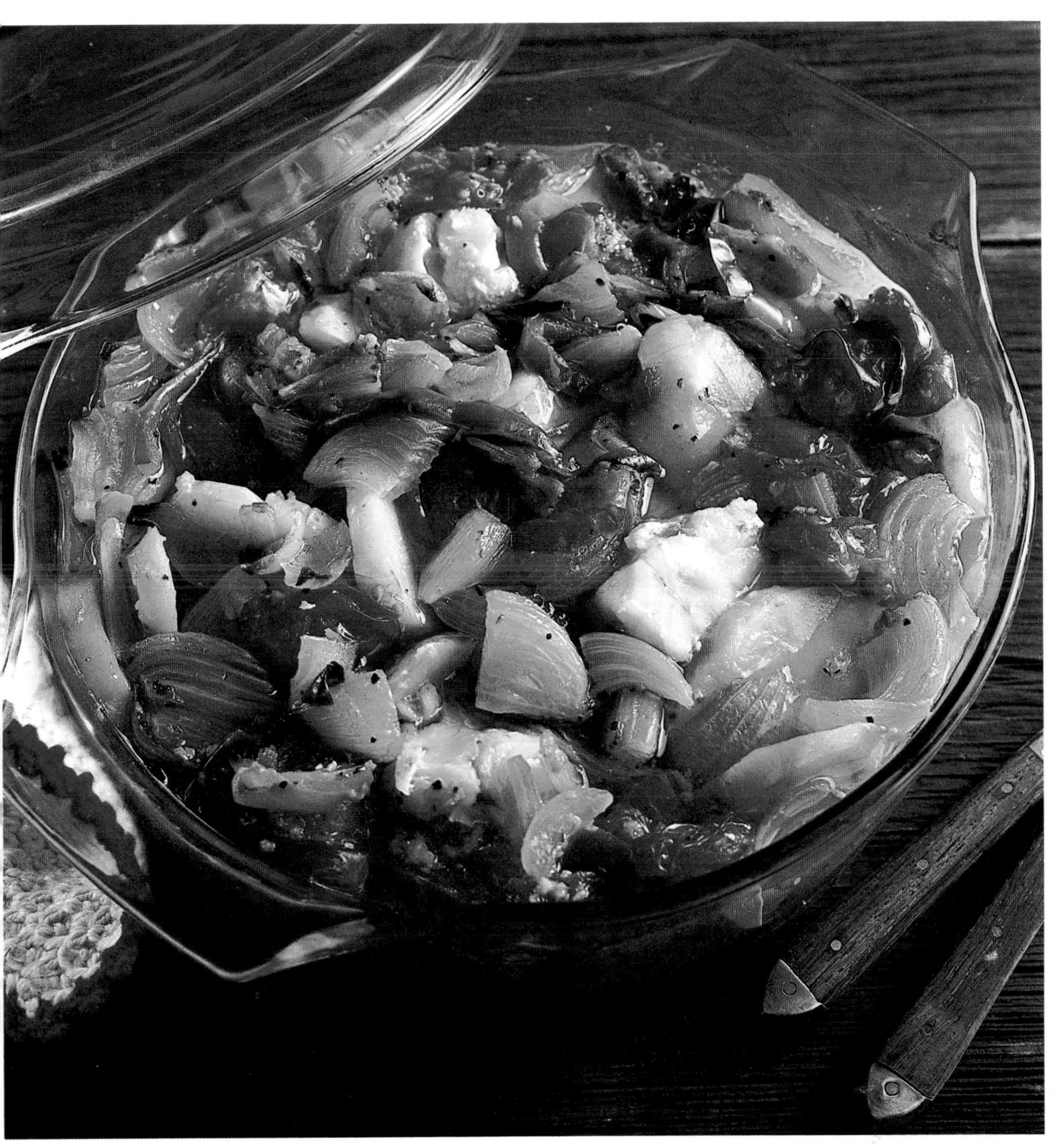

Cod Manuella

Serves 4

8 cod fillets
2½ tablespoons flour
salt and pepper
¼ cup oil
1 onion
1 large or 2 medium-sized zucchini
3 tomatoes
1 red pepper
1 tablespoon tomato paste
1 tablespoon wine vinegar
½ cup dry sherry
½ cup water
1 chicken stock cube
garlic salt
1 tablespoon chopped parsley

Clean and wash the cod fillets and cut into small pieces. Season the flour and sprinkle it over the fish.

Heat the oil in a flameproof dish and gently fry chopped onion, sliced zucchini, skinned and chopped tomatoes, seeded and sliced red pepper. When they are soft stir in the tomato paste, vinegar, sherry and water. Crumble in the stock cube and boil for 12 minutes, stirring from time to time. Place the fish fillets on top, season with salt and pepper and cover with a lid. Simmer gently on top of the stove for 12 minutes.

Pour into a serving dish and sprinkle with chopped parsley.

Fish Curry with Saffron Rice

Fish Curry with Saffron Rice

Serves

500g fish steaks such as flake or gemfish
150 mL combined milk and water
salt and black pepper
4 tablespoons butter or margarine
1 small onion
2 tablespoons flour
2 tablespoons curry powder, or to taste
150 mL dry white wine
1 tablespoon lemon juice
2 tablespoons sultanas
1 tablespoon mango chutney
1 tablespoon desiccated coconut
185g shelled prawns
1 small green pepper

Saffron rice:

¼ cup oil
1 small onion, chopped
1¼ cups of long grain rice
4 cups water
1 bay leaf
1 chicken stock cube
¼ teaspoon saffron or turmeric powder
salt and pepper
½ cup roasted peanuts

Wash and bone the fish steaks and place in a pan wit the milk and water. Add salt and pepper and 2 tablespoons of the butter. Bring to the boil and poac gently for a few minutes until the fish steaks are cooked but firm. Remove, reserving the stock, and cut the fish into bite size pieces.

Melt the remaining butter (2 tablespoons) in a pan, add the finely chopped onion and fry for a few minutes until translucent. Stir in the flour and curry powder and cook for 1 or 2 minutes. Make up the reserved fish stock to 2 cups by adding the wine and more water. Gradually blend this stock into the curry mixture. Cook stirring constantly until the sauce has boiled and thickened. Add the lemon juice, sultanas, chutney, coconut, prawns, cooked fish pieces, and the seeded and finely chopped green pepper. Heat through and spoon into a heated serving dish. Serve with saffron rice.

Saffron rice: Heat the oil in a frypan, add the onion and sauté for a few minutes. Stir in the rice and cook for 1 minute or until the rice is translucent. Put the water bay leaf, crumbled stock cube and saffron in a separate saucepan, bring to the boil and simmer for 5 minutes.

train and pour the stock into the pan with the rice, over and cook for a further 5 minutes.

ransfer the contents of the pan to a shallow venproof dish, cover with a lid or greaseproof paper nd bake in a moderate oven for 20 minutes. Season ne rice with salt and pepper and sprinkle with the oasted peanuts.

Trout in Red Wine

Serves 4

cleaned trout
tablespoons butter or margarine
¼ cups red wine
small onion
ouquet garni
clove garlic, crushed
alt and pepper
tablespoons flour
tablespoon tomato paste or purée
inch ground nutmeg
½ cup sour cream

Garnish:

4 button mushrooms
2 slices toast cut into 8 crescent moon shapes

Grease a large shallow casserole dish with half the butter and arrange the fish in the casserole. Cover with red wine and add chopped onion, bouquet garni, garlic and seasoning. Cover and bake in a moderate oven for 20 minutes.

Remove casserole from the oven and strain the wine stock into a bowl for later use. Place the fish side by side on a shallow serving dish. With a sharp knife cut across the exposed skin of the trout 5 cm above the tail and 4 cm below the head. Carefully peel away the skin between these points. Keep the fish warm.

In a saucepan melt the remaining butter (2 tablespoons) and stir in the flour to make a smooth paste. Stir in tomato paste or purée and nutmeg and gradually add the wine stock. Cover and simmer for 10 minutes. Blend in the sour cream and simmer, stirring continually, for a further half minute.

Pour the sauce over the hot trout. Place a mushroom cap in the eye of each trout and surround the fish with the crescents of toast.

Trout in Red Wine

VEGETABLES

The dishes in this chapter may be served as an accompaniment to meat courses but can stand alone as a main course equally well. Vegetable dishes are a boon to people on a tight budget and also make a healthy and refreshing change from meat meals.

Pulses (such as lentils and dried beans) are very high in protein which makes them an ideal substitute for meat. The casserole method is wonderful for pulses as most of them require lengthy cooking.

Ratatouille (*See page* 86)

Ratatouille

Serves 6

2 large eggplants
4 medium zucchini
½ cup flour seasoned with salt
oil for deep frying
¼ cup olive oil
1 onion, chopped
1 clove garlic, chopped
2 green peppers, seeded and cut in strips
4 tomatoes, skinned, seeded and chopped
2 tablespoons tomato paste
1 sprig mint leaves
pinch oregano or basil
salt and pepper

Peel the eggplants and cut slantwise into 2.5 cm slices. Cut the zucchini, unpeeled, into similar sized slices. Put the slices of both vegetables on a board, sprinkle them with salt and let stand for 30 minutes. Rinse, drain and dry the slices and dredge in a generous ½ cup flour, seasoned with salt. Deep fry for 1 minute. Drain and dry the fried slices and transfer to a casserole dish.

Heat the cooking oil and sauté the chopped onion gently for 2 minutes. Add the garlic and green pepper and fry for 2 minutes, stirring frequently. Add the chopped tomatoes, tomato paste, mint, oregano or basil, and a pinch of salt and pepper to taste. Cover and simmer gently for 10 minutes. Pour this mixture over the eggplants and zucchini in the casserole dish and mix them lightly together. Bake in a moderate oven for 20–30 minutes. Serve hot or cold.

Bacon, Cheese and Potato Bake

Serves 4

1 kg potatoes
125 g lean, rindless bacon rashers
1 clove garlic, crushed
125 g butter
2½ cups water
1 chicken stock cube
1 cup grated Gruyère cheese
salt and pepper
grated nutmeg
1 tablespoon chopped parsley

Peel and thinly slice the potatoes, wash and drain. Blanch rashers of bacon for 3 minutes in boiling water, drain and chop into small pieces. Dissolve the chicken stock cube in 2½ cups of boiling water. Divide cheese and put half aside for the topping. Prepare an ovenproof dish by rubbing around the inside with the crushed garlic and greasing the dish with half the butter.

Cover the bottom of the casserole with a layer of potatoes, then arrange alternate layers of bacon, cheese and potato slices. Sprinkle with salt and pepper and grated nutmeg. Pour over the chicken stock and bake in a moderate oven for 25 minutes. Remove, sprinkle with remaining grated cheese and dot with butter. Bake for a further 20 minutes until golden-brown. Sprinkle with chopped parsley and serve.

Carrot and Mushroom Casserole

Serves 6

1 kg carrots
250 g button mushrooms
1 small onion
2 tablespoons butter or margarine
1 tablespoon tomato paste
1½ cups of water
1 chicken stock cube
½ cup sherry
salt and pepper
pinch each of mace and oregano
1 tablespoon chopped chives and parsley

Wash mushrooms and trim the ends of the stalks. Peel and chop onion; slice carrots. Heat butter and gently sauté onion for 4 minutes until soft but not brown. Add carrots, tomato paste and water. Bring to the boil and simmer uncovered for 30 minutes. Crumble stock cube into the mixture and add sherry, salt and pepper, spices and mushrooms. Simmer for 10 minutes.

Place in a serving dish and sprinkle with chopped chives and parsley.

A delicious accompaniment for roast pork or lamb.

Carrot and Mushroom Casserole

Parsnip and Tomato Bake

Serves 4

500g peeled and sliced parnsips
4 tablespoons butter or margarine
1 medium onion, chopped
1 clove garlic, chopped
2 tomatoes
salt and pepper
2 hard-boiled eggs
1 tablespoon chopped parsley

Boil the parsnips in salted water until just tender. Drain.

Heat the butter in a pan and fry the onion for 4 minutes until tender but not coloured. Add the garlic and sauté gently for a further minute. Add the skinned and chopped tomatoes, parsnips and seasoning.

Transfer the mixture to a shallow ovenproof dish and bake in a moderate oven for 20 minutes. Serve sprinkled with the chopped eggs and parsley.

Bacon, Cheese and Potato Bake (*See page* 86)

Potato Hotpot

Serves 4

500g potatoes
1 onion
2 stalks celery
1 chicken breast
1 rindless bacon rasher
2 tablespoons butter or margarine
1 tablespoon oil
2 chicken stock cubes
4½ cups of water
salt and pepper
juice of half lemon
½ cup cream
1 tablespoon chopped parsley

Cut the potatoes, onion and celery into strips 5cm by 5mm. Skin the chicken breast and remove the bone. Cut chicken and bacon into thin strips.

Heat butter and oil in pan, add the vegetable and meat strips; cook, covered, for 5 minutes. Crumble stock cubes into water and add to pan. Bring to the boil and simmer for 20 minutes. Add seasoning and lemon juice. Stir in cream and boil for 2 minutes. Serve sprinkled with chopped parsley.

Braised Onions with Sultanas

Serves 4

500g small onions, all about the same size
1¼ cups of water
1 cup white wine vinegar
3 tablespoons olive oil
4 tomatoes, skinned
salt and freshly ground pepper
⅓ cup sultanas
1 bouquet garni
¼ teaspoon sugar

Peel the onions, leaving on the root ends. Boil the onions in a pan with the water, vinegar and olive oil. Simmer gently.

Slice the tomatoes thinly and add to the onions with a pinch of salt and pepper, sultanas, bouquet garni and sugar. Return to the boil and reduce heat. Cover and cook slowly for about 30 minutes, stirring occasionally.

Before serving remove bouquet garni. Can be served hot or cold. If serving cold chill for at least 2 hours.

Braised Onions with Sultanas

Eggplant and Pasta Casserole

Serves 6

1 eggplant, about 375g
250g noodles or macaroni
2 tablespoons oil
2 onions, chopped
1 green pepper
1 red chilli (optional)
1 clove garlic, crushed
3 tomatoes
½ cup corn kernels
1 ⅓ cups diced cooked beef
salt and pepper
2 tablespoons butter or margarine
4 tablespoons flour
2 cups beef stock
2 egg yolks
½ cup soft breadcrumbs
1 teaspoon chopped parsley
2 tablespoons melted butter

Slice the eggplant, salt and leave for 30 minutes. Rinse and dry. Meanwhile boil the noodles in salted water for about 10–12 minutes until just tender; drain.

Heat oil in a pan and fry eggplant slices until golden. Lift out, drain and set aside. In the same pan fry chopped onions, seeded and chopped green pepper, chilli slices, garlic, skinned and chopped tomatoes. Cook for 4 minutes, then mix in corn kernels.

In a greased ovenproof dish arrange ingredients in layers as follows: eggplant; diced beef seasoned to taste with salt and pepper; mixed fried vegetables; noodles.

Heat the 2 tablespoons of butter in a saucepan and stir in flour. Cook over a low heat for a couple of minutes. Add the beef stock gradually, stirring well, and pour the liquid over the lightly beaten egg yolks in a separate bowl. Stir briskly then return egg mixture to the saucepan and stir continually for 2 or 3 minutes over a gentle heat until thickened.

Pour the sauce over the noodles and bake in a moderate oven for 20–30 minutes. Sprinkle casserole with the breadcrumbs, chopped parsley and melted butter. Return to oven for 5 minutes or until the top is crisp and golden.

Eggplant and Pasta Casserole

Boston Baked Beans

Serves 10

550g dried haricot beans, soaked overnight
1.8 litres water
1 onion, finely chopped
1 tablespoon tomato paste
1 tablespoon dry mustard
1 tablespoon Worcestershire sauce
1 teaspoon salt
pinch ground cloves, or 2 whole cloves
1 tablespoon vinegar
2 tablespoons black treacle
100g bacon, cubed

Wash and drain the soaked beans and place them in a large pan with the water. Do not add any salt. Bring to the boil, reduce the heat and simmer for 45 minutes, removing any scum that rises to the surface. Set the oven at 150°C (300°F).

Transfer the beans and liquid to an ovenproof casserole and stir in the remaining ingredients. Cover the casserole and bake for 2 hours.

Remove the lid from the casserole and bake for a further 30 minutes. Serve hot.

Boston Baked Beans

Ribbon Bean Bake

Serves 4

1 onion, chopped
1 clove garlic, finely chopped
1 tablespoon olive oil
¼ cup chopped celery
1 tablespoon chilli sauce
½ cup tomato purée
¼ cup tomato paste
¼ cup red wine
½ teaspoon salt
¼ teaspoon pepper
¼ teaspoon oregano
¼ teaspoon basil
½ cup cooked butter beans
½ cup cooked chick peas
½ cup cooked red kidney beans
1 cup cooked soy beans
½ cup cooked lima beans
250g Mozzarella cheese
250g Ricotta cheese
Parmesan cheese

Heat oil and cook onion, garlic and celery 5 minutes. Add chilli sauce, tomato purée and paste, wine, salt, pepper, oregano and basil. Simmer 25 minutes.

Combine all beans and peas in a bowl.

Slice Mozzarella cheese thinly. Beat Ricotta cheese in a bowl until smooth. Place one third tomato sauce in bottom of medium-sized casserole. Spoon in one third bean mixture and spread on third Ricotta cheese over beans. Place one third Mozzarella cheese on Ricotta. Repeat layers twice and sprinkle finished casserole with Parmesan cheese.

Cover and bake for 30 minutes at 190°C. Remove cover and bake 10 minutes more to brown.

Zyldyk Casserole

Serves 4

250g spinach
2 carrots, sliced
1 large zucchini, sliced
1 large onion, sliced
175g cauliflower florets
175g white cabbage, shredded
25g butter
25g flour
150 mL skim milk
175g Edam cheese, finely grated
2 teaspoons curry powder
25g fresh white breadcrumbs

Celery and Onion Casserole *(See page 94)*

Zyldyk Casserole

EDAM

Set the oven at 190°C (375°F). Discard the stalks from the spinach. Place the spinach in a pan, cover and cook for about 10 minutes, shaking the pan occasionally.

Place the carrot, zucchini, onion, cauliflower and cabbage in a pan and cover with cold water. Bring to the boil, then drain, reserving 150 mL of the liquid. Place the vegetables in an ovenproof dish and arrange the spinach on top.

Melt the butter, stir in the flour and cook for 1 minute. Gradually add the reserved vegetable cooking liquid and milk. Bring to the boil and simmer for 2 minutes, stirring continuously. Stir in 100g of the cheese, the curry powder and seasoning to taste. Pour over the vegetables.

Combine the remaining cheese and breadcrumbs and sprinkle on top of the vegetables. Bake for 30 minutes. Serve hot.

Golden-topped Vegetable Casserole

Serves 4–6

1 eggplant
2 carrots
2 potatoes
2 onions
¼ cup olive oil
4 zucchini
4 tomatoes
2 cups okra, canned or fresh
¼ cup chopped parsley
2 teaspoons oregano
salt and pepper
¼ teaspoon nutmeg
3 cups mashed potato
½ cup grated cheese
2 eggs
½ cup milk

Slice eggplant, sprinkle with salt and allow to stand 30 minutes. Peel and slice carrots and potatoes. Plunge them into boiling water and simmer 5 minutes. Drain and rinse under cold water. Peel and slice onions. Rinse eggplant and pat dry.

Fry onions in heated oil until soft. Remove and fry eggplant until golden brown. Slice zucchini and tomatoes. Top and tail okra. In a deep casserole layer all vegetables, sprinkling each layer with a little parsley, oregano, salt, pepper and nutmeg.

Cover casserole and bake at 200°C (400°F) for 30 minutes. Combine mashed potato, cheese, egg yolks, milk and paprika until smooth and creamy. Beat egg whites until stiff and fold into potato mixture. Spoon over casserole and place in oven. Bake at 190°C (375°F) until top is golden.

Celery and Onion Casserole

Serves 4

1 head of celery
250g diced bacon
250g small onions
¼ cup oil
1 tablespoon tomato paste
2 chicken stock cubes
2 cups water
bouquet garni
salt and pepper

Trim celery and slice stalks into 10cm pieces; dissolve stock cubes in the 2 cups of water.

Heat the oil in a pan, add diced bacon and sauté for 4 minutes. Remove and add peeled whole onions, then the sliced celery. Cook for 5 minutes. Stir in the tomato paste and pour in the chicken stock; add bouquet garni. Season, replace bacon pieces and transfer mixture to an ovenproof dish. Cover and cook in a moderate oven for 35 minutes.

Carrot Casserole

Serves 4

2½ cups carrots, sliced
1 small onion, finely chopped
½ cup water
salt and freshly ground pepper
1 tablespoon honey
¼ cup soy grits
2 tablespoons dill, snipped
¼ cup sunflower seeds
1 egg lightly beaten
60g almonds, chopped

Place carrots, onion, water and salt into a saucepan. Bring to the boil, cover and simmer until carrots are just tender. Preheat oven to 180°C (350°F). Stir in all remaining ingredients except almonds. Pour into a shallow baking dish, sprinkle with almonds and bake 15 minutes.

Carrot Casserole

Index

Printed in Singapor